So eat, my darling

So eat, my darling

A guide to the yiddish kitchen

Recipes by Naf Avnon
Folklore by Uri Sella

Fell's Books Fill Your Needs

FREDERICK FELL PUBLISHERS, INC. NEW YORK

Edited by Ava Swartz
Designed by Magda Tsfaty
Photographs in color and black and white by Chanan Sadeh, Haifa;
front cover by Menuha Brafman.
Historical photographs from the archives
of YIVO Institute for Jewish Research, New York.

First published in Israel in 1977
by Tal International Publishing Company Ltd.
11 Alouf Sadeh Street, Givatayim, Israel.

For information address:
Frederick Fell Publishers, Inc.
386 Park Avenue South
New York, N.Y. 10016.

Library of Congress Cataloging in Publication Data
Avnon, Naftali.
So eat, my darling.
Includes index.
1. Cookery, Jewish. I. Sela, Uri. II. Title.
TX724.A93   641.5'67'6   77-3006
ISBN 0-8119-0282-X

Published simultaneously in Canada
by Thomas Nelson and Sons (Canada) Ltd.
81 Curlew Drive
Don Mills, Ontario M3A 2R1, Canada.

Made and Printed in Israel
by Peli Printing Works Ltd.

contents

Preface

Throughout the ages, the Jewish love of food has been celebrated in legend and lore. Food always played a vital role in the poor Jewish villages of Eastern Europe, and many beloved traditions have sprung from its preparation and consumption — whether for a lavish feast or simple peasant meal.

This book is meant to evoke the flavor and spirit of the Jewish kitchens of Eastern Europe. Some of the recipes included here are renown throughout the world; others are regional variations or little known specialties, but all reflect the traditional cuisine of a culture and lifestyle long gone. The accompanying folktales and anecdotes tell more about the zest and humor Eastern European Jews devoted to food.

Although rooted in the traditions of Eastern European Jews, all of the recipes have been tested and updated. Ingredients and procedures have been adapted for modern usage; some methods are detailed in easy-to-follow illustrations; all of the ingredients are listed in the order used, and step-by-step procedures simplify methods of preparation.

At the close of the book is a complete index and a conversion table of equivalent weights, measures and temperatures in the American and Continental (metric) system.

In keeping with the Jewish dietary laws, the recipes are kosher — which means that certain cuts of meat and types of fish have been omitted, and that dairy products never appear with meat recipes. A special section on the kosher kitchen explains the history of the *kashrut* laws and tells how to keep a kosher kitchen.

We would like to extend a special note of thanks to Mrs. Julia Grafman who spent countless hours coordinating the testers, updating the recipes, and offering invaluable practical suggestions. We are also grateful to the expert assistance of Mr. Joseph Sobol of Haifa, an international chef who created many of the holiday recipes and whose skilled hands prepared the dishes for photography.

Introducing the
Yiddish Kitchen

Most creative and interesting dishes originate in the kitchens of the poor which were always the homes of invention and combination. A prime cut of meat slung over the fire could always satisfy the rich, but the poor had to use their ingenuity. How, for example, could a chicken produce not one meal but three? Meat could be wrapped in dough to produce extra portions, vegetables could suffice for an entire meal and spices could camouflage the lack of expensive ingredients. This was where some of the most interesting gastronomic inventions of the French, Italian — and Jewish — kitchens were born.

Most of the Jews of Eastern Europe were very poor. A man who could feed his family was considered a happy man. While Marie Antoinette was telling the masses to "eat cake" the Jews coined their own adage: "Don't ask for honey cake if you have bread." Bread was regarded with great respect and mothers would teach their children to value every slice. During the week, the Eastern European Jew made do with a hunk of bread and a simple dish such as soup or potatoes, but on Shabbat and on holidays, the Jewish table was fit for a king. One worked all week to prepare for Shabbat and when a Jew wanted to indicate his sorry financial state, he would say, "I don't have enough for the Shabbat meal."

The Shabbat menu rarely varied, except according to the time and place. Every Shabbat table was adorned with at least two loaves of **challah**, a braided bread made from white flour and glazed with egg yolk to make the crust brown and shiny. The custom of two loaves of Shabbat **challah** dates back to the Biblical account of the heavenly **manna** which God provided for the Children of Israel. On weekdays, they were ordered to gather only enough **manna** for one day, but on the eve of Shabbat, they were commanded to gather two portions of bread for Friday and Shabbat. German Jews called them **brachas** because of the **bracha** or blessing said over them.

Fish was another essential item on the Shabbat table. The Talmud tells of the legend of "Joseph the Shabbat lover," a poor Jew who would go to any expense to honor Shabbat. One Friday morning, he bought the most succulent and expensive fish in the market and when he cut it open, he found a precious jewel in its belly.

In time, the custom of eating fish on Shabbat became sanctified to the extent that when a German Jew wanted to swear that he was telling the truth, he would say, "Let me not have fish for Shabbat if I speak not the truth."

Fish also played a role in the persecution of the Jews. During the Middle Ages Jews were frequently forbidden to buy fish because the anti-Semites believed that it magically increased the fertility of Jewish males. Another special Shabbat dish that graced Jewish tables at noontime on Shabbat was the famous cholent, a succulent stew made with meat, potatoes, beans and vegetables and simmered overnight. Since the observant Jew may not light a fire on Shabbat, a special dish had to be invented that could be put in the oven a day earlier and kept warm until lunchtime on the following day. So cholent came into being. Sometimes, kishke or knaydel were also added to the pot before it was stewed overnight.

Some say the name cholent originated with the French word chaud meaning hot and became schalet when the Jews wandered from medieval France to Germany. However, schalet means peel in German, and since there are no peels in cholent, many believe the phonetic similarity caused the change. Whatever its root, this famous stew ultimately became known as cholent in Eastern Europe. In addition to Shabbat dishes, the Jews developed their own holiday recipes. Special challoth were baked for Rosh Hashanah when it was the custom to eat sweets (usually an apple dipped in honey) to insure a sweet New Year. On the eve before the fast of Yom Kippur, tradition called for dumplings stuffed with meat, which were symbolic of God's compassion for his people. At the end of the fast, one sat down to a lavish festive meal, but not before drinking a cup of tea with a slice of lekach (honey cake). On Tu Bishvat, the fifteenth day of the month of Shevat, which Jewish tradition regards as Arbor Day, the Jews of Eastern Europe ate dried (and mostly imported) fruits reminiscent of the fruits of Israel: Figs, raisins and carobs. On Chanukah, it was customary to eat donuts filled with jam and potato latkes or pancakes. Purim was the time for meat dumplings and for triangular cakes filled with poppy-seeds known as homentashen. Pesach brought a unique menu to the Jewish table crowned with matzoth and traditional dishes, the most popular being matzo knaydlach (dumplings) made of a special flour which did not contain leaven. For the Shavuoth festival of the first fruits of the season, dairy foods, such as blintzes and cheesecake were traditional.

Of course, the above list is but a mere morsel of Jewish holiday food. Why were the Jews so obsessed with food? One recalls the story of Gabriel Pascal, the film producer who wanted to make a film of George Bernard Shaw's play, "Pygmalion." Pascal tried to impress the playwright with his artistic sensibilities, but Shaw only wanted to know how much money the producer was willing to pay. Finally, Pascal exclaimed in disgust: "I'm talking about art, and you're talking about money." To which Shaw replied: "That's perfectly natural. People talk about what they don't have."

The Jews talked about food because that was what they lacked. Jewish literature of Eastern Europe is chock-full of tasty dishes and festive meals described with the kind of passion usually reserved for erotic scenes.

Food was also the topic of many Jewish proverbs, whether as the main subject or as an analogy or metaphor for something else. For example, to talk some sense into a loafer, they would say, 'Roast pigeons don't fly into your mouth." For the backslider who shirked his responsibilities, the common rebuke was, "Eating you can do!" The meaning was clear — all he could do was eat. And when their problems were not as difficult as they seemed they would say, "Troubles with supper you can bear" — for the only serious trouble was hunger.

For Jews all over the world, food has always been a divine blessing and its consumption part of religious ceremony. There are blessings for many types of food and each meal is blessed twice, once before the meal and again afterwards, as stipulated in the Book of Deuteronomy: "And you shall eat and be full and you shall bless..." Amen.

In keeping with the Jewish dietary laws, the following symbols accompanying each recipe are used to separate milchig (milk) from flayshig (meat) dishes. Pareveh dishes contain neither dairy nor meat products.

 milchig

 flayshig

 pareveh

appetizers

appetizers

There is an old tale about a Roman emperor in the days of the Second Temple who once asked the sage, Rabbi Joshua ben-Hannaniah, "Why do your Shabbat dishes smell so wonderful?"
"We have one ingredient called Shabbat," replied the sage, which gives them that aroma."
"Give it to us too," said the Emperor.
"It only works for those who observe Shabbat" said Rabbi Joshua, "it's no use to anyone who doesn't."

Ground fish patties, Lithuanian style
(litvishe gefilte fish)

3 pounds fresh carp or pike,
filleted, with heads, bones and skin
3 medium onions, quartered
3 carrots, peeled and halved
2 eggs
3 tablespoons matzo meal or bread crumbs
¼ cup cold water
salt and pepper to taste
2 quarts Fish broth (see below)

1 The night before, place fillets in a shallow dish, salt lightly, cover and refrigerate overnight. Reserve the head, bones and skin for the broth.
2 The next day, put vegetables and fillets through fine blade of a meat grinder. Transfer to mixing bowl and add eggs, matzo meal, water and salt and pepper. Add additional water, if necessary, so that mixture is fluffy and slightly sticky to the touch.
3 Prepare the Fish broth.
4 Shape the fish mixture into 3-inch patties and gently place them in the simmering broth. Add enough water to cover patties, cover the saucepan with a tight-fitting lid and simmer 1 hour.
5 When patties are ready, turn heat off and cool them in the broth. Carefully remove with a slotted spoon. Strain broth and pour over patties. Garnish with carrots and onions from the broth and serve with Horseradish sauce (page 41). Serve either warm or cold; if served cold, cool broth until it jells.
Serves 6

Fish broth for gefilte fish
(fish-sohs)

head, bones and skin from carp or pike
3 medium carrots, sliced into 1/8-inch pieces
1 parsley root, peeled
1 celery root, scraped
2 onions, thinly sliced into rings
2 quarts cold water
salt and pepper to taste

Place all ingredients in a large kettle, bring to a boil, reduce heat and simmer 15 minutes. Adjust seasoning.

*A beggar went into a restaurant, ate and drank his fill but when they brought him the bill he told the owner,
"I haven't any money."
"What do you mean," fumed the owner. "You eat, you pay!"
"Take it easy," said the beggar. "I haven't any money just now, but I'll go out into the street and beg, and I'll bring you all I collect."
"How do I know you'll come back and pay?" mocked the owner.
"If you don't believe I'll come back, you can come with me, but if it's beneath your dignity to be seen with me, I'll stay here and you can go and collect yourself."*

●●●●●●●●●●

Shabbat without fish is like a wedding without dancing. (Folk-saying of French Jews).

●●●

How to prepare gefilte fish, Lithuanian style

1 *Prepare vegetables for stuffing.*
2 *Put vegetables and fish fillets through a meat grinder.*
3 *Add eggs, matzo meal and seasonings to mixture and blend well.*
4 *Shape into patties and place into simmering broth, adding enough water to cover.*

1
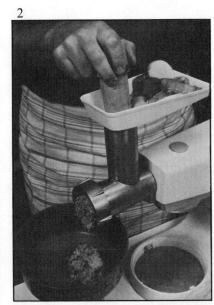

2

3

4

13

appetizers

Stuffed fish slices, Polish style
(poilishe gefilte fish)

Rabbi Menahem-Mendel
of Kotzk, one of the great
Hassidic Rabbis was once
asked why he never wrote
a book. The Rabbi replied,
"Let's say I do write a
book. Who is going to buy
it? My disciples will buy
it. And when will they find
time to read it? They are
busy the whole week try-
ing to make a living. That
leaves Shabbat. On Shab-
bat eve, they must first of
all go to the mikvah to
cleanse themselves, then
they must go and pray and
after that they have their
Shabbat feast. A man eats
fish, chicken soup, meat
and challah; he drinks
wine and chants the Shab-
bat songs. Only after that
does he have time to read
a book. So, he stretches
out on his bed. His
stomach is full of good
food and wine. He opens
the book, but his eyes
close and he falls asleep.
Now, tell me, I pray you,
what am I to write a book
for? To help my disciples
fall asleep?"

●●●

whole 3-pound carp or pike, cleaned, with head*
2 quarts Fish broth (see page 12)
1-pound carp or pike, filleted, with bones and skin
1 egg, lightly beaten
2 tablespoons matzo meal
1 medium onion, grated
2 medium carrots, grated
½ teaspoon brown sugar
salt and pepper to taste

1 The night before, cut the whole fish into 2-inch slices
  (keeping the head whole), salt lightly, cover and refrigerate.
2 The next day, prepare the Fish broth (page 12).
3 Put fillets through fine blade of a meat grinder. Mix with the
  remaining ingredients. Add enough cold water to the stuffing
  to form a sticky paste.
4 Place fish slices on a flat surface and fill with the stuffing.
  Carefully lower stuffed slices into simmering fish broth.
  Simmer 2 hours, cool in broth and carefully remove slices.
  Strain the broth and pour over the fish. Garnish with carrot
  and onion slices from the broth and serve with Horseradish
  sauce (page 41). Serve either warm or cold; if served cold,
  cool the broth until it jells.
Serves 4-6
* See illustrations on page 73.

One of the great
Hassidim, Rabbi Baruch,
used to say, "It is written
in the Bible that 'the
righteous eateth to satisfy
his soul, but the belly of
the wicked shall want.'"
On the face of it, this verse
is astonishing. Do the
wicked always go hungry?
Is not the exact opposite
usually true? Look again:
When a righteous man
receives a guest in his
home, he serves the finest
dishes and eats with him
(even if he is not hungry)
to make his guest feel
comfortable.
But when a wicked man
has a guest in his home, he
will not eat (even if he is
hungry) so that he will not
have to serve his guest a
meal.

Pickled fried fish
(marinierte gepregelte fish)

2 pounds pike or mackerel, cleaned*
1 teaspoon salt
dash of pepper
1 tablespoon chopped fresh parsley
1 tablespoon flour
1 egg, lightly beaten
5 tablespoons bread crumbs
2 tablespoons butter or margarine
1 cup cider vinegar
1 cup cold water
2 bay leaves
1 teaspoon unflavored gelatin

1 Cut fish into 1-inch pieces, rub with salt and pepper and
sprinkle with parsley. Cover and refrigerate 3 hours.
2 Dust fish with flour, dip in beaten egg and dredge in bread
crumbs. Melt butter or margarine in skillet and sauté fish.
Drain on absorbent paper towels.
3 In a small saucepan, bring vinegar, water and bay leaves to
a boil. Turn off heat and cool. Stir in gelatin.
4 Pack fried fish in a 1½-2-quart jar, pour vinegar mixture
over, cover tightly and refrigerate 2 days. Serve cold with
jelled sauce. May be stored in refrigerator 1 week.
Serves 6
* See illustrations on page 73.
Color plate facing page 16.

Whenever somebody in a rich family got married, the town beggars enjoyed a good dinner at the lucky house where a special table was laden with juicy meat, fat fish and other delicacies for them, so that they might eat and be merry. The poor used to eat as much as they could stuff in at these feasts, for who knew when they would again have the chance of eating such good food? They justified their guzzling by explaining verse 19 of Chapter 3 in the Book of Genesis: "In the sweat of thy brow shalt thou eat bread" as meaning "Eat hard, till you sweat from the effort."

Pickled sweet and sour fish
(ziess un zoyere marinierte fish)

2 pounds carp or pike, cleaned*
1 carrot, peeled and sliced
1 parsley root, peeled
½ teaspoon salt
dash of pepper

Pickling mixture

1 cup cider vinegar
½ cup water
1 small onion, sliced
½ cup brown sugar
2 teaspoons seedless raisins
2 bay leaves
1-inch piece ginger root
3 garlic cloves
½ teaspoon ground allspice
¼ teaspoon ground nutmeg
salt to taste

1 Cut fish into 1-inch pieces and put in saucepan along with carrot, parsley root, salt and pepper. Cover with water and boil 15 minutes until fish is tender but firm. Cool. Remove fish from broth and set aside.
2 Combine pickling mixture ingredients in a saucepan, bring to a boil and cool.
3 Pack cooked fish in a 1-quart jar, pour pickling mixture over, cover tightly and refrigerate 24 hours. Serve cold. Will keep in refrigerator 1 week.
Serves 6
* See illustrations on page 73.
Color plate facing page 16.

Pickled fish has many varieties. Pictured from top to bottom: Pickled herring with apples (page 21), Pickled fried fish in the jar (page 10) next to Fillet of Matjes in olive oil (page 18), Pickled sweet and sour fish (page 16).

White fish in aspic
(fish petchah)

2 pounds fresh carp, cleaned*
2 medium onions, chopped
1 tablespoon oil
2 cups boiling water
1 cup dry white wine
2 bay leaves
2 teaspoons salt
½ teaspoon pepper
2 envelopes unflavored gelatin

1 Wash carp and cut into 8 slices.
2 sauté onions in oil until golden brown.
3 Transfer onions to a 2-quart saucepan. Add boiling water, wine, bay leaves, salt and pepper. Bring to a boil again and add carp pieces. Reduce heat, cover and simmer 1 hour.
4 Remove from heat and let fish cool slightly in broth. Then carefully remove to a 2-quart mold with sides at least 2 inches high. Strain the broth.
5 Dissolve gelatin in ½ cup of strained broth, add to remaining broth, stir well and pour over carp slices in mold. Chill in refrigerator until firm. When ready to serve, unmold by immersing mold in hot water for a few seconds. Place on a large serving platter.
Serves 8
* See illustrations on page 73.

Calf's foot jelly (page 23) is traditionally served with lemon and hard-boiled eggs.

appetizers

A Hassid was once complaining to his Rabbi about the poor living he was making. "What about your health?" asked the Rabbi. "Do you have a good appetite?"
"My appetite is fine, thank God," replied the Hassid.
"Well then," said the Rabbi, "you're well off. Another Hassid visited me only yesterday and told me that his wife suffers from lack of appetite and that he has already spent over five hundred roubles on doctors and medication. Now, you go and work out how much money your appetite is worth."

●●●●●●●●●●●●

When you have no fish, make do with herring — it's also fish!

●●●

Herring baked in pastry leaves
(gehakte herring in bletterteig)

3 salt herrings
1 cup milk
1 package prepared pastry leaves
2 tablespoons olive oil
½ cup finely chopped dill pickle

1 Soak herrings in water to cover for 24 hours. Change water several times. Drain and fillet carefully. Marinate in milk for an additional 8 hours.
2 Remove pastry leaves from refrigerator at least 2 hours before using.
3 Drain fillets, rub them with olive oil and sprinkle with pickle.
4 Preheat oven to moderate (350°F).
5 Place a sheet of pastry leaves on a flat surface and cut to three times the size of each fillet. Wrap the fillets in the pastry leaves, tucking in the pastry on all sides. Place on a well-greased cookie sheet or pan and bake about 45 minutes or until crust is golden brown.
Note: Pastry leaves are sometimes called strudel leaves and are available at most food stores. They usually must be defrosted before use. Unused portions can be stored in the freezer.
Serves 6

Fillet of matjes in olive oil
(matyes herring in masslienes ail)

2 matjes herrings
1 cup milk
2 small onions, sliced into thin rings
5 peppercorns
olive oil to cover

1 Soak matjes herring in water to cover ½ hour. Rinse and soak in milk for an additional hour.
2 Fillet the herrings and cut into 2-inch slices.
3 Place in clean 1-pint jar. Add onions, peppercorns and oil to cover. Close with tight-fitting lid. Chill in refrigerator 1 week before serving.
Serves 4
Color plate facing page 16.

18

How to fillet a herring
1 *Cut off head and slit on backside from head to tail, cutting to the backbone.*
2 *Open fish and scrape meat from bones.*
3 *Insert knife under backbone and carefully separate meat from bones.*
4 *Lift out and discard entire backbone.*

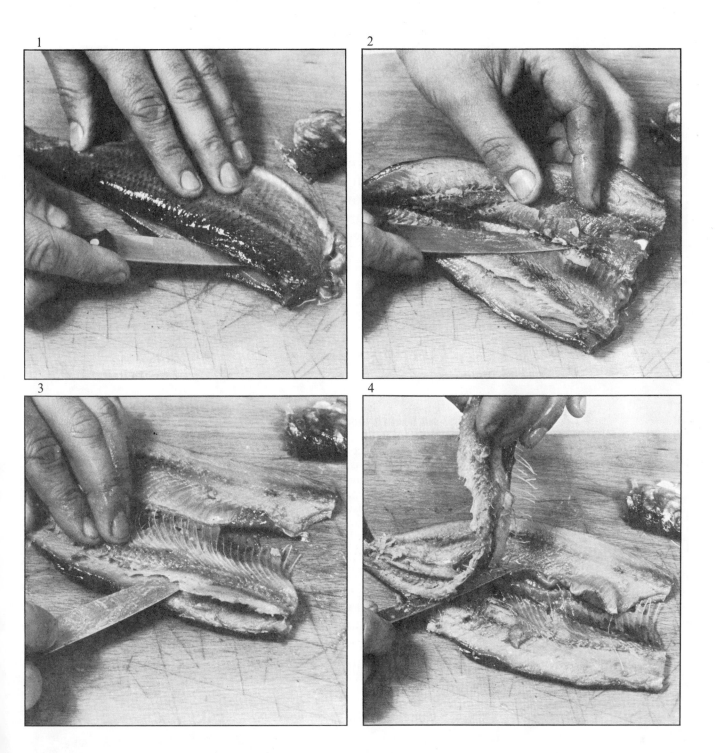

Severely wounded after a shoot-out with a rival gang, the Jewish criminal dragged himself back to his parents' house. "Mama!" he gasped, barely able to stand. Back came the answer: "First eat my son, then we'll talk. . ."

●●●

Chopped herring
(gehakte herring)

2 large salt herrings
1 slice dark bread
1 tablespoon lemon juice
diluted in 2 tablespoons water
2 onions, grated
2 green apples, peeled, cored and grated
2 hard-boiled eggs, chopped
½ teaspoon cinnamon
½ teaspoon sugar
freshly ground pepper to taste

1 The night before, soak herrings in water to cover and refrigerate. Change water frequently.
2 The next day, soak bread in diluted lemon juice. Drain, clean and fillet herrings (see illustrations on page 19). Cut into pieces and put through fine blade of a meat grinder.
3 In a deep mixing bowl, mash ground herring, bread slice and remaining ingredients until smooth and well blended. Adjust seasonings. Serve on lettuce leaves or spread on dark bread.
Serves 4-6

Herring salad
(herring salat)

3 salt herrings, filleted*
1 pound potatoes, boiled and diced
2 small onions, coarsely chopped
½ cup mayonnaise
½ cup sour cream
1 tablespoon prepared mustard
lemon juice to taste
salt and pepper to taste

1 Soak the herring fillets overnight in water to cover. Drain and cut into ¼-inch strips.
2 Mix the herring with the potatoes and onions.
3 Combine the mayonnaise, sour cream, mustard, lemon juice and salt and pepper. Add to the herring mixture and mix. Adjust seasonings and garnish with chopped parsley, if desired.
Serves 6
* *See illustrations on page 19.*

For a woman who was always crying, people would say: She's salting the fish with her tears.

●●●●●●●●●

The poor eat when the rich are sick.

●●●●●●●●●

You don't have to salt the herring or spread fat on the grieben.

●●●

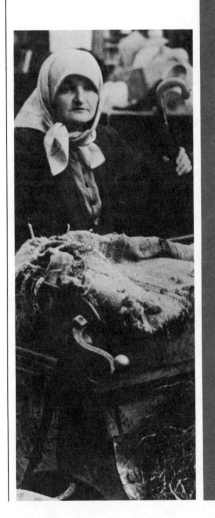

Pickled herring with apples
(marinierte herring mit eppel)

6 salt herrings
1 cup vinegar
2 bay leaves
10 peppercorns
1 teaspoon sugar
2 medium apples, peeled, cored and sliced
2 medium onions, sliced in thin rings
2 cups boiling water
3 tablespoons mayonnaise
1½ cups sour cream
1 teaspoon prepared mustard

1 The night before, soak herrings in water to cover, changing water several times. The next day, clean, fillet (see illustrations on page 19) and cut into 1-inch slices.
2 In a small covered saucepan, boil vinegar, bay leaves, peppercorns and sugar 5 minutes. Pour into heat-proof mixing bowl and set aside to cool.
3 In a second mixing bowl, mix apples and onions and pour boiling water over. Steep 10 minutes and drain.
4 Add mayonnaise, sour cream and mustard to the vinegar mixture.
5 In a 2-quart jar, alternate layers of herring with layers of the apples and onions. Pour vinegar-mayonnaise marinade over herring and close with a tight-fitting lid. Cool and chill in refrigerator for 3-4 days before serving.
Makes about 24 slices
Color plate facing page 16

Dill pickles
(gezoierte iggerkes mit krip)

2 pounds small cucumbers
2½ cups water
1 tablespoon salt
2 garlic cloves
fresh dill and celery leaves

1 Wash and clean cucumbers thoroughly. Pack tightly together in a 2-quart jar.
2 Mix water, salt and garlic and pour over cucumbers until jar is almost full. Cover with dill and celery leaves and close with a tight-fitting lid. Place in a sunny spot for 1 week before serving.
Makes 2 quarts

Egg and horseradish dip
(chrayn mit ayer eintunkechtz)

4 hard-boiled eggs
1 cup sour cream
½ cup freshly grated horseradish
1 tablespoon prepared mustard
1 tablespoon lemon juice
1 teaspoon sugar
1 teaspoon salt

Chop the eggs finely and combine with the remaining ingredients.
Makes about 1½ cups

Egg and scallion spread
(ayer mit griene tzibbeles)

6 hard-boiled eggs, mashed
3 scallions, sliced finely
1 tablespoon mayonnaise
1 tablespoon sour cream
dash of pepper

Mix all ingredients together. May be served as a spread on fresh rye bread or as a dip.
Serves 4-6

Calf's foot jelly
(petchah)

1 calf's foot
1 onion
2 sprigs parsley
1 teaspoon thyme
1 teaspoon rosemary
salt and pepper to taste
4 garlic cloves, crushed
hard-boiled eggs

1 Have butcher chop calf's foot into small pieces. Wash thoroughly and place in a heavy 2-quart saucepan. Add onion, parsley, thyme, rosemary, salt and pepper. Cover with water, bring to a boil and simmer, covered, about 3 hours or until bones separate easily from the cartilage. Cool.
2 Discard bones and onion. Reserve broth. Remove cartilage and chop finely. Strain the broth, mix with cartilage, add garlic and pour into square pan. Adjust seasoning and cool until partially jelled. Skim off and discard surface layer of fat and refrigerate overnight or until jelled. Before serving, cut into squares. Garnish with slices of hard-boiled egg.
Serves 8
Color plate facing page 17.

Chopped liver
(gehakte layber)

4 tablespoons chicken fat
1 large onion, chopped
1 pound liver (beef, calf or chicken), sliced
2 hard-boiled eggs
salt and pepper to taste

1 Melt 1 tablespoon of the chicken fat in a medium skillet and sauté the onions until transparent.
2 Preheat broiler. Salt and broil liver a few minutes on each side. Rinse.
3 Grind the livers with the eggs, using the medium blade of a food chopper or a hand chopper. Mash the remaining 2 tablespoons of chicken fat with the liver and egg, adding the seasoning to taste.
Serves 6

Rabbi Mordecai of Lachovitz was a Hassidic Rabbi. Desperately poor, his wife and family used to complain and weep bitterly because they had nothing to eat.
But one day a visitor went into Rabbi Mordecai's room and found him in a happy mood.
"How can you be so happy," he asked, "when your wife and children are crying of hunger?"
"It suits them to cry," replied the good rabbi, because they expect me to give them food. But who am I? I'm just flesh and blood. But I have nothing to worry about, for when I raise my eyes to the Holy One, Blessed be He, I don't doubt for one moment that He will desert me — He will provide."

Sweet and sour meat balls

(ziess un zoyere gehakte flaysh)

½ cup chopped onions
1 tablespoon oil
1 egg
1 ½ pounds ground beef
2 tablespoons bread crumbs
½ teaspoon salt
1/8 teaspoon pepper
6-ounce can tomato paste
1 cup tomato sauce
2 tablespoons lemon juice
2 tablespoons brown sugar

1 Sauté onions in oil until golden brown.
2 Place in mixing bowl and add egg, ground meat, bread crumbs, salt and pepper. Mix well and form into small 1-inch balls.
3 In a 2-quart saucepan, combine tomato paste, tomato sauce, lemon juice and brown sugar. Add meat balls and water to cover. Bring to a boil, reduce heat and simmer, covered, 1 hour.
Serves 8-10

soups

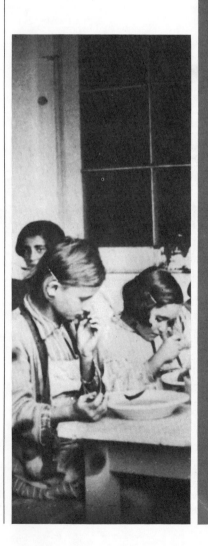

Cauliflower soup

(kalifior-zup)

1 large cauliflower head
6 cups cold water
½ pound potatoes, peeled and quartered
2 teaspoons butter
1 cup milk
dash of nutmeg
salt and pepper to taste

1 Separate and discard tough outer leaves from cauliflower. Wash cauliflower thoroughly and place in large kettle or saucepan with the water. Bring to a boil, cover and simmer until tender, about 15 minutes. Remove cauliflower and set aside.

2 Add remaining ingredients to water, bring to a boil, cover and simmer until potatoes are soft. Remove from heat and cool.

3 Separate and set aside a few florets from the cauliflower for garnish. Cut remaining cauliflower into small pieces, add to soup and mix well. Put entire mixture through an electric blender or fine sieve. Return to kettle, add reserved florets and reheat before serving.

Serves 6

*Rabbi Abraham-Abbale,
of Vilna was once teaching
his students Torah when
the door suddenly opened
and a young girl came in,
wearing an apron.
"Rabbi," she asked,
"what am I to cook for
lunch?"
Without a moment's
hesitation, the Rabbi
answered seriously, "You
can cook vegetable soup
and noodles."
The girl thanked him and
ran out the door, leaving
his students gaping in
amazement.
"Don't you understand?"
laughed the Rabbi, "You
can see that she's working
in the kitchen, and from
her question I gathered
that she had asked her
mistress what to cook for
lunch. Her mistress was
either busy or irritable so
she told her sarcastically
to 'go and ask the Rabbi,'
but this simple girl didn't
realise she was being
sarcastic, so she came to
ask me."*

● ● ●

Celery root soup
(tzelery-zup)

1 medium celery root, peeled and diced
½ pound potatoes, peeled and thickly sliced
2 tablespoons butter
4 cups cold water
2 cubes vegetable bouillon
1 tablespoon flour
salt and pepper to taste
4 tablespoons sour cream, room temperature
croutons (optional)

1 In a 2-quart saucepan, lightly sauté celery root and potatoes
in 1 tablespoon of the butter. Add the water, bouillon cubes,
flour and salt and pepper. Cover, bring to a rolling boil and
simmer 40-50 minutes.
2 Turn off heat and stir in second tablespoon of butter. In a
small bowl, combine sour cream with 3 tablespoons of the
broth and gradually stir into soup. Serve immediately
garnished with croutons.
Serves 4-6

soups

Shalom Aleichem tells a
story about a village Jew
whose wife had a baby
boy. On the eighth day
after the birth, which was
a Friday, they were to
have the Brith — the
circumcision ceremony,
where at least ten Jews
must be present to form a
minyan. The trouble was
that there were only nine
Jews in the whole village
and that even included the
Mohel, the circumciser.

The happy father ran to
the railway station —
maybe God would be good
to him, and he'd find a
Jewish traveler who would
agree to attend the Brith.
And indeed, God was
good. He found a Jewish
traveling salesman, who
had gone into the station
canteen to eat something.
He tugged at his sleeve
and said, "Reb Jew, I can
see that you are hungry.
You won't find much here
to eat. Come to my house
and you'll get a good
lunch, a fine pot roast and
fresh challah."

The man looked at him as
if he was crazy, but when
the happy father explained
what it was all about and
also promised him chicken
soup with lokshen and the
finest cherry wine, the Jew
agreed to go, on condition
that he could catch the
next train.

The ceremony went well
and the guest sat down,
ate and drank and did not
even notice how time was
passing. Suddenly, as dusk
fell, he got up and wanted
to go.

Potato soup
(kartoffel-zup)

3 large potatoes, peeled and diced
1 carrot, peeled and sliced
1 onion
1 parsnip
2 stalks celery
2 cups water
salt and pepper to taste
1 teaspoon butter
1 cup milk

1 Place potatoes, carrot, onion, parsnip, celery and water in a large kettle. Bring to a boil, cover and simmer until potatoes are soft, about 35 minutes.
2 With a slotted spoon, remove and discard onion, parsnip and celery.
3 Before serving, add butter and milk and reheat.
Serves 4-6.

Potato-leek-milk-soup
(kartoffel mit prash milch-zup)

1 pound potatoes, peeled and thinly sliced
½ pound leeks, washed and chopped
1 tablespoon butter
2 cups milk
2 cups cold water
salt and pepper to taste

Place all ingredients in a 3-quart kettle, cover, bring to a rolling boil and simmer ½ hour or until potatoes are done.
Serves 4-6

*"Where are you going?"
asked his host. "Are you
going by train on Shabbat?
It looks as if God himself
wanted you to spend
Shabbat with us, to taste
my wife's gefilte fish.
You've never tasted such
fish in all your life!"*

*In short, the guest stayed
and ate his fill of the fish,
the chicken soup with*
lokshen *which he liked,
the roast meat and the
dessert, not to mention the
brandy before the fish —
and also after! Then he
said, "I must admit, I
haven't enjoyed a Shabbat
meal like this in a very
long time."
"In that case," said his
host, "stay and see what
my wife will serve
tomorrow for our Shabbat
lunch." And it really was
worth it.*

They ate gehakte *herring,
then chopped eggs with
scallions, and after that
garlic-flavored* petchah
with challah, *and then a
succulent* cholent *with a
plump* kishke, *a rich* kugel
and a golden carrot
tzimmess *and finished off
the feast with a compote
made with juicy, fat
prunes. After each dish,
the guest lavished praise
upon his host.*

*After he had smacked his
lips over the last morsel,
his host said, "That's
nothing. You just wait and
taste the* babke *that my
wife makes for the
conclusion of Shabbat."*

Cold tomato soup

(kalte tomatten-zup)

2 pounds tomatoes
6 cups cold water
1 medium onion, sliced
2 stalks celery with leaves, chopped
2 sprigs parsley, chopped
2 sprigs fresh dill or ½ teaspoon dried dill weed
dash of ground or grated nutmeg
pinch of sugar
salt and pepper to taste
1 cup sour cream

1 Blanch tomatoes by covering with boiling water. Steep 5 minutes and peel off skin.
2 Place all ingredients except sour cream in a 3-quart kettle, cover and gently boil ½ hour or until tomatoes are very soft. Cool.
3 Gradually stir in sour cream and pass entire mixture through a sieve or electric blender.
Refrigerate and serve cold.
Note: May be stored in refrigerator several days.
Serves 8-10

soups

"Oh, I'll be a long way away by then," laughed the contented traveler. But as luck would have it, there was no train that evening and so he stayed and ate five big slices of the moist, delicious cake and drank three glasses of wine. Before going to sleep, he made his hosts promise to wake him early the next morning so that he could catch his train.

The next morning he woke up very late and was very annoyed that his hosts hadn't called him in time. However, they calmed him down and told him that it was the custom to make a festive meal on the third day after the Brith. *And so, he stayed.*

While they were sipping their after-dinner brandy, the proud father said, "So far, you have only tasted our meat dishes, but this evening my wife is making a spread of dairy dishes such as you have never eaten in all your life. If you stay and eat with us this evening, I swear I'll wake you in good time tomorrow morning and you can go in peace. . ." Well, he was persuaded, and the latkes *and cheese* kreplach *were simply delicious!*

Early the next morning his host took him to the railway station. As they began to say good-bye, the father suddenly said, "Of course we will make our farewells, but first we have to make our accounts."

Cold cherry soup
(kalte karshen-zup)

2 pounds fresh cherries, pitted
2 cups water
1 ½ cups dry red wine
½ cup sugar
1 teaspoon grated orange rind
4 cloves

Place all ingredients in a 2-quart saucepan. Bring to a boil, cover and simmer 15-20 minutes. Chill. Remove cloves before serving.
Serves 6

Bulgarian cucumber soup
(bulgarishe iggerke-zup)

6 medium cucumbers, peeled and diced
salt to taste
1 cup fresh minced dill
4 garlic cloves, minced
3 cups yogurt
½ cup sour cream
2 tablespoons olive oil
6 ice cubes

1 Place cucumbers in a large serving bowl and sprinkle with salt. Mix in dill, garlic, yogurt and sour cream. Streak the oil over the top.
2 Just before serving, float the ice cubes on top of the soup.
Serves 6

"What accounts, all of a sudden?" cried the guest. "The bill for everything you ate and drank," replied his host. "Don't you realize that fish cost money, and so does the babke that you raved about, and we don't get cheese and butter for nothing either."

The traveler was furious. "You thief! You cheat" he shouted. "You got hold of me in the railway station, invited me to the Brith, begged me to stay — and now you want to rob me!" "What are you shouting for?" returned his host. "Let's go to the nearby town and visit the Rav who will settle the matter. We'll abide by whatever he says."

The man agreed and so the two of them got into a cart and soon reached the Rav's house. Angrily, the traveler poured out his story and when he had finished the Rav said, "Well, I've heard one side, so now let's hear the other."
"I have nothing to add," said the host. "All that he said is true. But I'd like to ask him one thing — did he praise the fish or not? Did he eat the cholent or not? And after the kugel and the kreplach, did he or did he not smack his lips with pleasure?"

The Rav listened, looked over the bill and decided that the guest was to pay for all he had eaten and drunk.

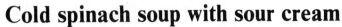

Cold spinach soup with sour cream
(kalte shpinat-zup mit smetene)

1 ½ pounds spinach leaves
3 scallions, thinly sliced
6 cups cold water
2 teaspoons salt
2 tablespoons lemon juice
½ teaspoon sugar
2 eggs
1 cup sour cream

1 Thoroughly wash spinach leaves, chop and place in 3-quart kettle with scallions and water. Add salt and bring to a boil. Reduce heat and, while liquid is simmering, add lemon juice and sugar. Cover and simmer 15-20 minutes. Remove from heat and cool.
2 Beat eggs in a bowl and gradually add 1 cup of the broth stirring constantly to prevent curdling. Stir this mixture into the soup and chill.
3 Just before serving, mix in sour cream, stirring constantly until well blended. Serve cold.
Serves 6

Rice and milk soup
(reiz un milch-zup)

1 cup white rice
3 cups boiling salted water
1 tablespoon butter or margarine
salt to taste
2 cups milk
cinnamon and sugar to taste

1 In an uncovered 2-quart saucepan, cook rice with boiling salted water and butter until rice is tender and water is absorbed.
2 Add salt and stir in milk. Cover and simmer 5-10 minutes. Serve hot with cinnamon and sugar to taste.
Serves 4

soups

When they left his house, the man took out his wallet and held out the money, but his host refused to take it. "Money?" he cried, "What bill? Do you think I'm a highway robber to take money from a Jew who spent Shabbat with me; a man I invited myself and who did me a favor and came to the Brith and made up the minyan?"

●●●●●●●●●●●

The man looked at his host as if he was completely mad. "If you didn't want money," he asked testily, "what did you give me a bill for, and why did you drag me to the Rav?"
"Don't you understand?" replied his host, "I simply wanted you to see for yourself what a fine Rav we have here in town."

●●●

Ukrainian cabbage and vegetable borsht
(ukreinishe kroit-zup)

½ pound soup meat, cubed
½ pound soup bones
2 quarts water
2 medium onions, chopped
1 small celery root, peeled
1 parsley root, peeled
¼ of a small white cabbage, shredded
5 medium beets, peeled and sliced
1 tablespoon lemon juice
2 tablespoons tomato paste
1 bay leaf
pinch of allspice
salt and pepper to taste

1 In a heavy 3-quart kettle, sear the soup meat quickly on all sides. Add soup bones and water and bring to a rolling boil. Skim the foam from the surface.
2 Add remaining ingredients, bring to a boil again, reduce heat and simmer gently, covered, 2-3 hours. Adjust seasonings before serving.
Serves 8-10
Color plate facing page 32.

Meat soup
(flaysh-zup)

1 pound lean meat
½ pound marrow bones
2 quarts cold water
2 small carrots, peeled and sliced
1 onion
2 stalks celery with leaves
2 sprigs parsley
2 sprigs fresh dill or ½ teaspoon dried dill weed
salt and pepper to taste

1 Place meat, bones and water in a large kettle or saucepan, cover and boil gently 1 hour. Skim off foam during cooking.
2 Add remaining ingredients, bring to a boil and simmer, covered, until meat is tender, about ½-1 hour. Remove onion, celery, parsley and fresh dill before serving.
Note: For a soup with a darker color, lightly sear onion by holding it over an open flame on a long fork until slightly browned before adding to soup.
Serves 6

Soups are a staple of the Yiddish kitchen. Pictured from top to bottom: Ukrainian cabbage and vegetable borsht (page 32), Hearty vegetable soup (page 36) and Mushroom and barley soup (page 37).

Meat and cabbage borsht

(flayshiger kroit borsht)

2 tablespoons chicken fat or oil
2 medium onions, chopped
½ pound soup meat, cubed
½ pound soup bones
2 cups shredded white cabbage
1 pound sauerkraut
½ cup tomato juice
2 quarts water
1 tablespoon lemon juice
3 medium apples, peeled, cored and cubed
2 tablespoons sugar
½ teaspoon pepper

1 In a heavy pot or Dutch oven, heat fat or oil and sauté onions until golden. Add meat and sear on all sides.
2 Add soup bones, white cabbage, sauerkraut, tomato juice and water. Bring to a boil and skim off foam from the surface. Reduce heat, cover and simmer 2 hours.
3 Add lemon juice, apples, sugar and pepper. Cover and simmer an additional 45 minutes.
Serves 8-10

Goulash soup

(gulash-zup)

3 medium onions, chopped
2 tablespoons chicken fat or oil
½ pound beef, cubed
3 tomatoes, skinned and puréed
¼ cup tomato paste diluted in ¼ cup water
1 teaspoon sweet paprika
¼ teaspoon marjoram
¼ teaspoon dried dill weed
salt to taste
hot paprika to taste
1 quart water
4 large potatoes, peeled and cubed

1 In a heavy pot, sauté onions in fat or oil until translucent. Add beef and cook over low flame 20 minutes.
2 Add puréed tomatoes, diluted tomato paste, sweet paprika, marjoram, dill, salt and hot paprika. Add water and bring to a boil. Cover and simmer 1 hour.
3 Correct seasonings, add potatoes, cover and simmer 1 hour longer.
Serves 4-6

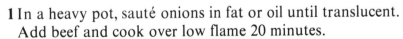

Marinated pot roast (page 42) goes especially well with Red cabbage in wine (page 84) garnished with Dumplings (page 110).

Before the Russian revolution, the government once ordered the appointment of an official rabbi in every town and city. The men appointed were usually learned scholars, but were not regarded as religious authorities by the Jewish public.
A woman once came to one of these Rabbis, bringing a slaughtered chicken. She was not sure it was kosher. "I have a question to put to you, Rabbi," she said.
"Doctor, if you please," the official corrected her. On hearing this, the woman took her chicken and wanted to leave. "Why are you going?" the government-appointed Rabbi asked.
"My chicken is dead," she said: "A doctor's no use!"

Golden chicken soup

(goldene hiener-yoich)

4-5 pound stewing chicken with gizzard, heart and neck
3 quarts cold water
1 large onion, halved
1 large carrot, peeled and sliced
2 stalks celery with leaves, coarsely chopped
1 parsley root, peeled and coarsely chopped
1 bay leaf
6 peppercorns
1 tablespoon salt

Method for frozen chicken

1 Place frozen chicken with gizzard, heart and neck in a large soup kettle. Add remaining ingredients, cover, bring to a rolling boil and continue boiling 10-15 minutes. Reduce heat and simmer 2 hours.
2 Remove chicken, strain soup and refrigerate overnight.
3 The next day, remove top layer of fat (which can be added to *schmaltz* jar, page 64).

Method for fresh or defrosted chicken

1 Rinse chicken and cut into serving pieces. Pull off and remove skin and excess fat (which can be used to make *schmaltz,* page 64).
2 Place skinned chicken pieces along with gizzard, heart and neck in a large soup kettle filled with the water. Cover and bring to a rolling boil and continue boiling 15-20 minutes. Uncover and skim foam from surface. Reduce heat, cover and simmer 15-20 minutes.
3 Add remaining ingredients, cover and continue simmering 1½-2 hours.
4 Remove chicken and strain soup. Correct seasonings.
Serve with Matzo meal dumplings (page 111) or Kreplach (page 116).
Serves 10-12
Color plate facing page 105.

Bean soup
(fassoles-zup)

¾ cup dried white beans
2 pounds marrow bones
3 small potatoes, peeled and quartered
2 medium carrots, peeled and sliced
1 medium onion
1 small celery root, peeled
salt and pepper to taste

1 Soak beans in water to cover overnight.
2 The next day, drain and rinse beans. Place in 4-quart kettle with marrow bones. Add cold water to cover, bring to a rolling boil and skim foam from surface. Reduce heat, cover and simmer 2 hours.
3 Add vegetables and salt and pepper to taste. Bring soup to a boil again, reduce heat and simmer 1 hour. Discard onion and celery root before serving. Discard bones, if desired. This soup tastes even better the next day.
Variation: Remove bones and put soup through blender. Add bones and reheat before serving.
Serves 6

soups

Lentil soup
(linzen-zup)

2 cups dried lentils
2 small onions, chopped
1 tablespoon chicken fat or oil
1 carrot, sliced
2 stalks celery with leaves, chopped
1 parsley root, scraped
2½ quarts water
salt and pepper to taste

1 Soak lentils in water to cover 6 hours or overnight.
2 In a large kettle, sauté onions in chicken fat or oil until golden brown. Drain and rinse lentils and add to kettle along with carrots, celery, parsley root and water. Add salt and pepper to taste, bring to a boil and simmer, covered, 1½ hours.
Serves 8-10

Hearty vegetable soup
(gemieze-zup)

½ cup dried navy or haricot beans
6 cups cold water
1 pound marrow bones
1 large tomato
2 medium potatoes, peeled and cubed
3 large carrots, peeled and sliced
1 medium onion, thinly sliced
1 zucchini, peeled and sliced
2 stalks celery with leaves
2 sprigs parsley
2 sprigs fresh dill or ½ teaspoon dried dill weed
2 tablespoons barley
salt and pepper to taste

1 The night before, soak beans in water to cover.
2 Fill a soup kettle with the water and add bones. Cover, bring to a boil and cook 20 minutes. Remove foam from surface. Drain beans, add to kettle and continue cooking 40 minutes.
3 Meanwhile, blanch the tomato by covering with boiling water. Steep 5 minutes, drain and peel off skin. Add peeled tomato to the kettle along with the remaining ingredients. Cover, bring to a rolling boil and simmer 1 hour. Remove celery, parsley and fresh dill before serving.
Serves 6
Color plate facing page 32.

A Jew was once stuck in a small village late one Friday and was unable to get home before Shabbat. There was one Jew living there, so the traveler asked him how much it would cost him to spend Shabbat in his house.

"Ten roubles," said the man.

"That's an awful lot," the visitor grumbled, "can't you reduce the price?"

"No way!" said he. "That's the price, take it or leave it."

As he had no alternative, the traveler agreed and spent the whole Shabbat there. The finest dishes were served at the meals and he ate and drank to his heart's content.

On Saturday evening he took out his pocket-book and wanted to pay.

"God forbid!" said his host "What kind of man do you think I am — to take money from a Jew who spent Shabbat in my home?"

"Then why did you first insist on my paying and such a high price too?" he wondered.

"Simple," replied the village Jew. "I wanted you to eat and drink as much as you liked, like a rich man who has paid a fortune for his meals."

●●●

Mushroom and barley soup
(krupnik)

½ cup dried lima beans
½ cup dried mushrooms
1 pound soup meat with bones
2 quarts water
2 tablespoons chicken fat or oil
1 large onion, chopped
1 cup barley
1 carrot, peeled and sliced
salt and pepper to taste

1 The night before, soak lima beans in water to cover.

2 The next day, drain lima beans and set aside. Soak mushrooms in water to cover 1 hour.

3 Meanwhile, place meat and bones in large kettle, add water and bring to a brisk boil. Remove foam from surface, add drained lima beans, reduce heat and simmer, covered, 1 hour.

4 In a small skillet, melt the chicken fat or oil and brown the onions. Add to kettle.

5 Drain mushrooms and add to kettle along with barley and sliced carrot. Add salt and pepper to taste, bring to a boil again and simmer, covered, 1 hour.

Serves 8-10

Color plate facing page 32.

soups

In **Germany: A Winter's Tale,** *the famous poet Heinrich Heine wrote that when he finally visited his home town after thirteen years, his elderly mother clapped her hands and said, "Oh, my son! Thirteen years have passed. You must be very hungry!"*

●●●

Calf's foot soup
(petchah-zup)

2 calf's feet
3 quarts cold water
1 teaspoon salt
½ teaspoon ground pepper
1 onion
2 garlic cloves, crushed
2 stalks celery with leaves
2 sprigs parsley
2 sprigs fresh dill or 1 teaspoon dried dill weed

1 Have butcher chop calf's feet in 2-inch pieces. Wash thoroughly with boiling water. Fill a large kettle with the cold water and add calf's feet, salt, pepper and onion. Bring to a rolling boil, reduce heat, cover and simmer 2 hours. Cool.

2 Remove bones and discard, reserving marrows and cartilage. Strain the broth and return to kettle with garlic. Chop cartilage and return with marrows to broth. Refrigerate 3-4 hours or until mixture jells.

3 Skim off and discard top layer of fat from jelled broth. Reheat until broth liquifies.

4 Add celery, parsley and dill, adjust seasoning and bring to a boil. Cover and simmer ½ hour. Discard celery, parsley and fresh dill (if used) before serving. Serve piping hot to avoid jelling.

Serves 6

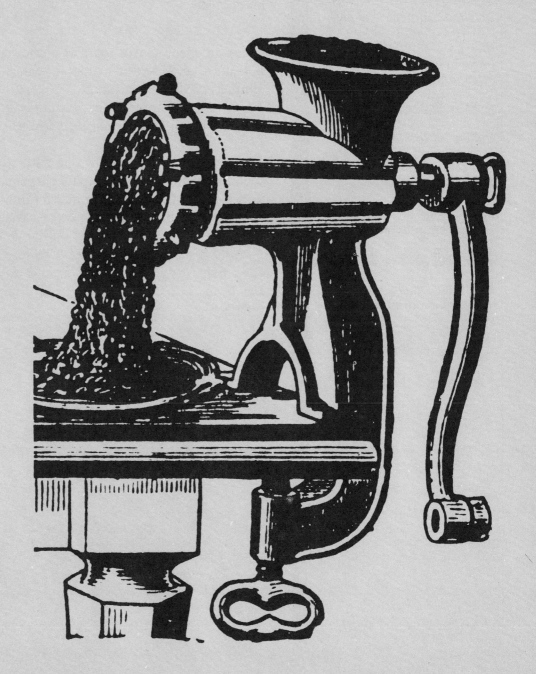

meats

meats

Beef with horseradish
(flaysh mit chrayn)

2 pounds brisket or soup meat
1 medium carrot, peeled and sliced in half lengthwise
1 medium parsley root, peeled and sliced in half lengthwise
1 small celery root, peeled and halved
1 medium onion or 1 leek
2 tablespoons margarine
1 tablespoon flour
4 tablespoons fresh grated horseradish
1 tablespoon cider vinegar
1 teaspoon sugar
salt and pepper to taste
bread crumbs

1 Place the meat, carrot, parsley and celery roots and onion in a 4-quart kettle, cover with cold water, bring to a boil and simmer, covered, 1½ hours.
2 Remove meat from broth, place in baking dish and set aside. Reserve broth and vegetables.* Preheat oven to moderate (350°F.).
3 In a medium skillet, melt fat and stir in flour until well blended. Add horseradish, vinegar, sugar, salt and pepper and 1 cup of the broth. Simmer 5 minutes. Pour over meat and top with bread crumbs. Bake 15-20 minutes or until top is brown. To serve, slice beef and pour sauce over.
* *For a zesty soup that serves 4, remove the vegetables from remaining broth, chop or put through a blender and return to the broth.*
Serves 6

Boiled meat with horseradish sauce
(gekochte flaysh mit chrayn)

2 quarts water
3 pounds beef brisket
2 carrots, peeled and chopped
1 onion

2 stalks celery with leaves, halved
salt to taste
Horseradish sauce (see below)

1 In a heavy pot or Dutch oven, bring water to a boil and add meat. Bring to a boil again and continue boiling while removing foam from surface.

2 Add vegetables and salt, cover and simmer 1-1 ½ hours. Remove meat from broth* and cool. Cut into serving slices and serve with Horseradish sauce (see below).

Horseradish sauce

1 tablespoon sugar
1 teaspoon salt
½ cup water
½ cup vinegar
½ pound horseradish, peeled and grated

Mix together the sugar, salt, water and vinegar. Add grated horseradish. Adjust sugar and salt to taste.

* *Reserve broth for another use.*

Serves 4-6

A poor Jew stood in the street begging for alms. "For pity's sake, give me a few pennies for a cup of coffee," he cried.

A wealthy Jew passed and gave the beggar some money. A little later, he went into a restaurant and saw the beggar drinking a glass of wine and enjoying a large plate of soierbraten with red cabbage.

"Aren't you ashamed of yourself," he rebuked the beggar, "begging for alms and then spending the money on expensive delicacies?"
"I don't understand you," said the beggar. "Before, when I had no money I couldn't eat soierbraten. Now, when I have, I'm not allowed to. When can I?"

●●●●●●●●●●●

Hershele Ostropoler went into a restaurant and ordered golooptchy, but when the juicy stuffed cabbage rolls were put before him, he changed his mind for some reason and said, "Bring me some lungen instead, please. It's the same price, isn't it?" The waitress took the stuffed cabbage rolls away and brought him a steaming plate of stewed lung. Hershele cleaned his plate and got up to go.
"You haven't paid for the lungen, sir," said the waitress.
"Why should I pay for it?" asked Hershele, "I gave you the golooptchy back for it."

Marinated pot roast
(soierbroten)

2 pounds beef shoulder
3 tablespoons matzo meal flour seasoned with salt and pepper
2 tablespoons oil
1 cup marinade
1 cup water
½ teaspoon sugar

Marinade
1 cup water
1 cup dry red wine or wine vinegar
1 carrot
1 onion, studded with cloves
1 garlic clove
½ tablespoon salt

1 Mix the marinade ingredients together and pour over meat. Cover and refrigerate 24 hours.
2 Remove meat from marinade and rub with seasoned matzo meal flour. Strain and reserve marinade. In a heavy pot or Dutch oven, heat the oil over a high flame and sear the meat on all sides.
3 Add 1 cup strained marinade, water and sugar to pot. Bring to a boil, cover and simmer 1½-2 hours or until meat is tender. Add additional water if necessary.
Serves 4-6
Color plate facing page 33.

"In that case, pay for the golooptchy." "Why should I?" he said, "I didn't eat it."

●●●

Beef stew
(gedempte flaysh)

2 pounds stewing beef, cubed
salt and pepper to taste
flour
3 tablespoons margarine or oil
2 medium onions, chopped
2 garlic cloves, crushed
1 green pepper, chopped
1 cup chopped celery with leaves
2 tablespoons fresh chopped parsley
1 teaspoon paprika

1 Sprinkle beef with salt and pepper and dredge in flour.
2 Heat margarine or oil in a heavy skillet or Dutch oven and brown meat on all sides. Remove meat and set aside.
3 Add onions, garlic, pepper and celery to skillet and sauté until tender. Return meat to skillet, sprinkle with parsley and paprika and add water to cover. Bring to a boil, cover and simmer about 2½ hours or until meat is tender.
4 Mix 1 tablespoon flour with 1 tablespoon water, add to stew and simmer 5 minutes longer. Adjust seasonings. Serve with steamed rice or boiled potatoes.
Serves 6

Rabbi Jacob Krantz once visited a rich and learned Jew to ask for alms for the poor. In his usual manner, he began by discussing some modern interpretations of the Torah in order to get down to business — the donation. The trouble was that the rich man went on talking about the Torah and disregarded all his hints and efforts to change the subject.

"I'll tell you a parable," said Rabbi Jacob, "about a prince who once sailed to an island where there were no onions. He took some onions out of the hold of his ship, gave them to the natives and explained that onions added a fine flavor to many dishes. They tried them and liked them and decided to express their gratitude by giving the prince a magnificent gift of gold and silver. When he returned from his voyage, the prince gave a banquet and told what had happened on the island.

Another prince heard the story, was filled with envy and thought, 'If there's no onion on that island, there is surely no garlic there either.'
So he set sail for the island and sure enough, they had no garlic, and he gave them a basketful, explaining how much it improves the flavor of many dishes. Again, they tried them and enjoyed them very much and decided that one good deed deserved another and gave

Shabbat stew
(cholent)

1 cup dried lima beans
3-4 tablespoons chicken fat or oil
3 medium onions, diced
2 ½ pounds chuck
8 medium potatoes, peeled and quartered
½ cup barley
salt and pepper to taste
1 tablespoon flour
2 tablespoons paprika

1 The night before, soak lima beans in water to cover.
2 The next day heat 2 tablespoons of the fat or oil in a heavy pot or Dutch oven and sauté onions over a high flame until transparent. Melt remaining fat, add meat and sear quickly on all sides.
3 Place potatoes around meat and add barley. Drain lima beans and add. Season with salt and pepper to taste, sprinkle with flour and paprika, barely cover with water and bring to a rolling boil.
4 Reduce heat, cover pot with tight-fitting lid and simmer 3 hours. Shake occasionally. Lift cover to check if more water is needed (cholent should be moist). Place covered cholent in very slow oven (225°F.) overnight, about 10 hours. Pot must be tightly covered at all times.
Note: *Cholent* is traditionally accompanied by *Kishke* (page 45). Place unbaked *Kishke* in cholent pot before stewing overnight.
Serves 6
Color plate facing page 49.

him — a basketful of onions!"
On concluding his tale, Rabbi Jacob said, "I tell you words of wisdom from the Torah not so that you will give me words of wisdom in return, but that you should return the favor in silver and gold."

●●●●●●●●●●●

Meat and fish are fine on Shabbat, but they're not bad any other day either.

●●●

Stuffed derma
(gefilte kishke)

2 feet of beef casing
¼ cup chicken fat
1 medium onion, minced
¾ cup flour
salt and pepper to taste
2 tablespoons bread crumbs
boiling salted water

1 Wash and clean the beef casing inside and out. Scrape off the fat with a dull knife. Cut into three 8-inch lengths. Sew up one end of each section.
2 Preheat oven to moderate (350°F.).
3 In a small skillet, melt the chicken fat and sauté onions until lightly browned.
4 In a mixing bowl, sift together the flour and salt and pepper. Add the bread crumbs and the melted chicken fat with the onions. Mix well and loosely stuff each section of beef casing with the mixture to allow for expansion while cooking. Sew up the other end. Shake and rinse off any flour from the surface.
5 Immerse in boiling water for 3-5 minutes and drain.
6 Arrange derma in a shallow greased baking dish and bake 1½-2 hours or until well browned. Baste frequently with the pan drippings.
Variation: *Kishke* is traditionally served with *Cholent* (page 44) or carrot *tzimmess* (page 48) and is usually cooked in the same pot. For this procedure, follow steps 1-5 of the above recipe, then either stew overnight with *cholent* or bake in casserole dish with *tzimmess*.
Serves 6
Color plate facing page 49.

meats

Sweet and sour meat stew
(essig flaysh)

1 large onion, minced
2 garlic cloves, minced
2 tablespoons oil
4 pounds stewing beef, cubed
2 bay leaves
salt and pepper to taste
1 ½ cups boiling water
2 tablespoons vinegar
2 tablespoons brown sugar
2 tablespoons tomato paste
½ cup seedless raisins

1 In a heavy pot or Dutch oven, sauté onions and garlic in oil until golden brown.
2 Add a few pieces of meat at a time and brown well on all sides.
3 Mix together remaining ingredients, pour over meat and bring to a boil. Cover, reduce heat and simmer 2 hours. Serve over rice, noodles or boiled potatoes.
Serves 8-10

"Then give me anything you have - maybe a bit of vursht?"

"I suppose you want Warsaw vursht?" *she inquired.*

"Yes, alright, Warsaw vursht."

"If so, you can please go to Warsaw and eat it there. Where do you think we get Warsaw vursht *from? Maybe you would like some* petchah?"

"Alright," he said wearily, "bring me some petchah."

"Sorry, we only have it on Shabbat!"

"So give me whatever you have — herring, a piece of meat, an omelet — whatever you have, because I'll soon die of hunger," he entreated.

"What a strange man!" the restaurant owner mused. "He'd like to eat everything. . ."

Smoked meat and cabbage stew
(geroicherte flaysh eingekocht mit kroit)

4 tablespoons oil
2 medium onions, coarsely chopped
1 pound red cabbage, shredded
1 pound sauerkraut, drained
¾ cup tomato paste
2 cups cold water
½ pound pastrami, diced
½ pound smoked tongue, diced
½ pound frankfurters, diced
½ pound *kabanos* sausage, sliced*
1 cup *grieben* (page 64), optional**
1 tablespoon sweet paprika
salt and pepper to taste

1 Heat oil in a large skillet and sauté onions until golden. Add cabbage and cook 10 minutes longer. Reduce heat, add sauerkraut and simmer 30 minutes.

2 Dilute tomato paste in the water and add to skillet along with remaining ingredients. Season to taste and continue cooking on a low flame 2 ½ hours, adding water if necessary to keep stew moist.

May be served over noodles sprinkled with caraway seeds. Stew improves with age and will keep in the refrigerator 7-10 days.

Serves 8

  * *Kabanos is a long, thin Rumanian-style dry sausage. Any dry sausage, including salami (diced), may be substituted.*

** *Grieben adds extra zest and makes this dish absolutely authentic.*

Color plate facing page 48.

A Jewish housewife once lent her neighbor an earthenware cooking pot. After some time, the woman returned the pot, but it was cracked. The owner of the pot summoned her neighbor to the Rabbi so that he could judge the case. Finally, the Rabbi asked the defendant what she had to say. "First, when I borrowed the pot it was already cracked," she announced. Secondly, when I returned the pot it was whole. Thirdly, I never borrowed any pot from her!"

● ● ●

Meat and carrot casserole
(flayshiger mayeren-tzimmess)

2 pounds beef brisket
salt and pepper to taste
6 medium carrots, peeled and sliced
1 tablespoon chicken fat or oil
1 medium onion, diced
2 tablespoons flour
½ cup brown sugar
¼ teaspoon cinnamon

1 In a heavy oven-proof pot or Dutch oven, sear the meat on all sides over a high flame. Season with salt and pepper to taste. Add water to cover, put on a tight-fitting lid and bring to a rolling boil. Reduce heat and simmer 1 ½ hours.
2 Add carrots and continue simmering an additional ½ hour. Pour off 1 cup cooking liquid and set pot aside.
3 Preheat oven to moderate (350°F.).
4 In a separate saucepan, heat fat or oil, add onions and sauté until lightly browned. Add flour and mix until smooth. Slowly pour in the cooking liquid, stirring constantly as mixture thickens. Add brown sugar, cinnamon, and salt and pepper to taste, and continue stirring until gravy is smooth and thick. Pour over meat and carrots and bake 45 minutes-1 hour or until top is well browned.
Variation: Add *Kishke* (page 45) to meat and carrots in step 4. Pour gravy over and bake as directed.
Serves 4-6

A traditional Cholent (page 44) is made with Kishke (page 45) and served with Challah (page 130).

▶

Prune, potato and meat casserole
(flayshiger tzimmess mit kartoffel un floymen)

1 tablespoon chicken fat or oil
1 medium onion, thinly sliced
1 pound beef brisket
½ pound dried prunes
1 pound small new potatoes, peeled and halved
½ cup brown sugar
2 tablespoons flour
½ teaspoon cinnamon
dash of nutmeg

1 In heavy pot or Dutch oven, heat fat or oil, add onions and sauté until golden. Remove onions and set aside.
2 Sear brisket in pot until well browned. Add sautéed onions and water to cover. Put on tight-fitting lid, bring to a boil and simmer 1 hour.
3 Put prunes and potatoes in a deep bowl. Add sugar, flour sifted with cinnamon and nutmeg to the bowl. Moisten with 2 tablespoons of liquid from the meat in kettle, mix well and arrange around meat. Replace lid and cook over a low flame 1 hour.
Serves 6

Goulash
(gulash)

2 pounds stewing beef, cubed
flour seasoned with salt and pepper
2 tablespoons oil
2 medium onions, chopped
6-ounce can tomato sauce
4 pounds potatoes, peeled and quartered
2 garlic cloves, crushed
1 teaspoon sweet paprika
Salt and pepper to taste

1 Dredge beef cubes in seasoned flour on all sides.
2 In a heavy saucepan, heat oil and sauté onions until golden brown. Add beef cubes and brown well on all sides. Add tomato sauce, potatoes, garlic, paprika and salt and pepper. Add water to barely cover and bring to a boil. Cover and simmer 1½-2 hours or until meat is very tender.
Serves 6

Smoked meat and cabbage stew (page 47) is an adaption of an old Polish dish which was usually served after a hunt.

meats

began his speech. He told of Bontche's hard life, of his miserable childhood, about his wicked stepmother who used to starve and beat him, about the hard work he did and the poor wages he was paid and about the hunger and cold he had suffered and yet, he had always kept silent and had never complained, not about other people nor of God.

He remained silent when he was cheated and when he was hurt, when his wife deserted him and left him their baby, and when the boy grew up and threw his father out of the house. Even when he lay in pain, dying in the hospital, when he could have cried out, then too, he was silent.

When the defending angel concluded his short speech, it was the prosecuting angel's turn to speak, but he only said:
"Gentlemen, he was silent — I too will be silent!"
And then, in the vaults of heaven the sweet and gentle voice of God was heard, "Bontche, my son, you were silent throughout all your sufferings. There is not a spot in your body which does not ache — and you were silent. In the world down there they did not know how to appreciate your silence but here, in the true world, you will receive your reward! We shall not judge you. Ask whatever your heart desires, and it shall be yours."

Meat loaf
(klops)

½ cup boiling water
2 tablespoons seasoned bread crumbs
1 garlic clove, crushed
½ teaspoon hot paprika
1 small onion, diced
½ pound ground beef
½ pound ground veal
1 egg
salt and pepper to taste

1 Preheat oven to moderate (350°F.).
2 Pour boiling water over bread crumbs, garlic and paprika. Add onions, beef, veal and egg and mix thoroughly. Season with salt and pepper to taste.
3 Place in a greased loaf pan. Even out surface and bake 1 hour.
Serves 4

Meat loaf with eggplant
(klops mit sinias)

2 large onions, chopped
2 tablespoons chicken fat or oil
1 pound eggplant, peeled and cubed
1 pound ground beef or lamb
2 eggs, separated
1 tablespoon bread crumbs
salt and pepper to taste

1 Preheat oven to slow (300°F.).
2 In a heavy skillet, sauté onions in fat or oil until golden brown. Add eggplant and sauté until tender. Transfer to deep bowl.
3 Add ground meat, egg yolks, bread crumbs and salt and pepper and mix well.
4 Beat egg whites until stiff and gently fold into meat mixture.
5 Grease a loaf pan and add meat mixture. Even out surface. Bake, uncovered, 1½-2 hours.
Serves 6

Then Bontche Schveig raised his bashful eyes and asked, "Truly?"
"Truly!" God replied. "Everything in heaven is yours. Choose and take whatever you wish — it is all yours."
"In that case," meekly smiled Bontche, "I want a hot roll with fresh butter every morning."

The angels hung their heads in shame and the prosecutor's laughter echoed throughout heaven.

●●●

Meat patties
(gemollene flaysh shnitzel)

1 onion, chopped
4 tablespoons chicken fat or oil
1 cup bread crumbs
1 teaspoon salt
½ teaspoon ground pepper
½ cup boiling water
1 pound chopped beef or lamb
1 egg, well beaten
2 garlic cloves, crushed

1 Sauté onions in 2 tablespoons of the chicken fat or oil until golden brown. Add 1 teaspoon of the bread crumbs, salt and pepper. Blend ingredients thoroughly. Add boiling water and stir. Remove from heat.
2 In a mixing bowl, blend together the chopped meat, egg and garlic. Add onion mixture and blend well.
3 Pour remaining bread crumbs into a shallow plate. Wet hands and form meat mixture into patties. Dredge on both sides in the bread crumbs.
4 Heat remaining 2 tablespoons of fat or oil in a large skillet. Fry the patties over a medium flame until golden brown on both sides.
Serves 4

Potted meat balls
(eingekochte flaysh kolen)

1 ½ pounds ground beef
1 egg
1 tablespoon bread crumbs or matzo meal
1 cup minced onions
1 tablespoon sweet paprika
salt and pepper to taste
2 tablespoons oil
2 garlic cloves, minced
2 carrots, peeled and sliced
3 potatoes, peeled and quartered
½ cup water

1 Combine beef, egg, bread crumbs, ½ cup of the minced onions, paprika and salt and pepper. Mix well and form into 1-inch balls.

2 In a large skillet, sauté the remaining ½ cup onions in oil. Add garlic and carrots. Add meat balls and brown on all sides. Add potatoes and water, correct seasonings and simmer gently, covered, 1-1 ½ hours. Serve over rice.
Serves 6

One of the great Hassidim, Rabbi Menahem-Mendel of Kotzk once read the following passage from the Bible to his disciples, "And the Children of Israel also wept again and said, 'Who shall give us meat to eat?' " (Numbers, Chapter 11, verse 4). Then the Rabbi asked rhetorically; "Why were the Children of Israel so angry with Moses in the desert? Why did they demand meat when they had manna? Each person could taste whatever dish he wanted when he ate the manna, so why should they insist on meat? Because the Children of Israel were not satisfied with taste alone . . . they wanted real meat."

●●●

Stuffed cabbage leaves I
(golooptchy)

boiling salted water
1 large cabbage head
3 onions, minced
2 tablespoons oil
1 pound ground beef
¼ cup raw rice
1 egg, beaten
½ teaspoon ground nutmeg
salt and pepper to taste
6-ounce can tomato paste
1 tablespoon brown sugar
juice of 1 lemon
1 teaspoon sweet paprika
2 cups cold water

1 Remove core from cabbage. Trim and separate leaves. Cook leaves in boiling salted water 5 minutes. Drain. (See illustrations on page 55).
2 Sauté onions in oil until golden brown and transfer to a mixing bowl. Add ground beef, rice, egg, nutmeg and salt and pepper. Mix well.
3 Place 2 heaping tablespoons of the stuffing on each cabbage leaf, roll and tuck in on all sides. Place rolls in a large saucepan.
4 In a separate bowl, mix together the tomato paste, brown sugar, lemon juice and paprika. Add 2 cups water, correct seasonings and pour over cabbage rolls. Bring to a boil, reduce heat and simmer, covered, 2 hours.
Makes about 12 cabbage rolls

Stuffed cabbage leaves II
(golooptchy)

1 large cabbage head
boiling salted water
3 tablespoons oil
½ cup chopped onions
1 garlic clove, minced
1 pound ground beef
2 cups cooked rice
½ cup seedless raisins
3 tablespoons fresh minced parsley
½ teaspoon thyme
1 teaspoon salt
black pepper to taste
2 cups tomato sauce
1 cup chicken soup
1 bay leaf

1 Remove core from cabbage. Trim and separate leaves. Cook leaves in boiling salted water 5 minutes and drain.
2 Preheat oven to moderate (350°F.).
3 Heat the oil in a large skillet and add onions and garlic. Sauté until onions are transparent. Set onions aside. Brown meat in skillet and add rice, raisins, parsley, thyme, salt, pepper and ¼ cup of the tomato sauce. Mix well and cook additional 5-7 minutes.
4 Place 2 tablespoons of the filling on each cabbage leaf. Roll and tuck in ends. Arrange rolls in a casserole dish.
5 In a small saucepan, bring the chicken soup, remaining tomato sauce and bay leaf to a boil. Pour over cabbage rolls and bake 1 hour. Discard bay leaf before serving.
Makes about 12 cabbage rolls

How to prepare stuffed cabbage leaves

1 - 2 *Remove core. Separate and trim leaves.*

3 - 4 *Cook leaves in boiling salted water for 5 minutes. Remove and drain.*

5 *Place stuffing at top of each leaf and roll up while tucking in sides.*

6 *Spoon sauce over cabbage rolls and bake 2 hours.*

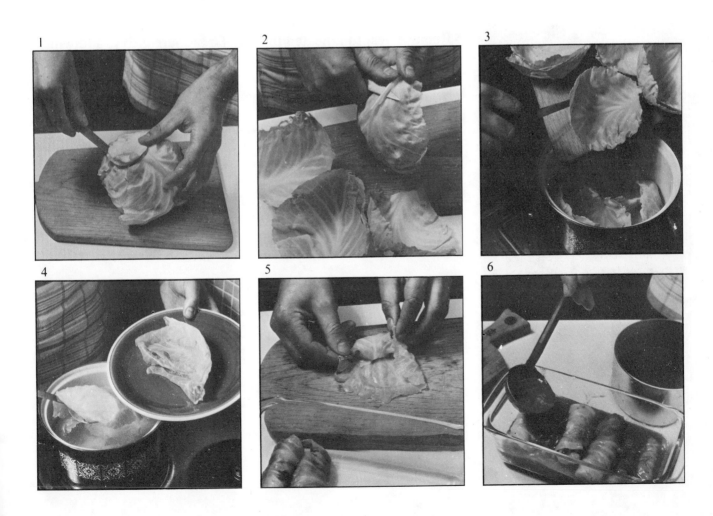

Veal breast with kasha stuffing
(kalbsbrust gefilt mit kashe)

4-pound veal breast
3 garlic cloves, crushed
paprika
1 onion, chopped
1 tablespoon oil or margarine
1 cup uncooked buckwheat (kasha)
salt and pepper to taste
1 cup water

Gravy
¼ cup dry white wine
½ cup boiling water
salt and pepper to taste

1 Have butcher cut a pocket in the veal breast. Rub with garlic and sprinkle with paprika.
2 Preheat oven to slow (300°F.).
3 In a heavy skillet, sauté onions in oil or margarine until golden brown. Add kasha and stir constantly until toasted. Season with salt and pepper to taste, add water and cover. Reduce heat and simmer gently 15 minutes or until kasha is soft.
4 Stuff kasha mixture into veal pocket, transfer to a roasting pan, cover and roast 2 hours. Remove cover and roast an additional ½ hour.
5 Remove veal to a heated platter. To prepare gravy, add wine, boiling water and salt and pepper to pan juices. Mix well and pour over stuffed veal breast.
Serves 4-6
Color plate facing page 65.

Liver with onions

(layber mit tzibbeles)

3 large onions, sliced
2 tablespoons chicken fat or oil
1 pound beef or calves' liver*
salt and pepper to taste

1 In a skillet, heat fat or oil and sauté onions until translucent.
2 Cut liver into 1-inch slices and quickly toss in skillet until all sides are well browned, about 2 minutes. Sprinkle with salt and pepper and serve immediately.
Serves 4

Stewed liver

(eingedempte layber)

3 onions, chopped
2 tablespoons chicken fat or oil
1 ½ pounds beef liver*
salt and pepper to taste
1 cup beef or chicken broth
½ pound potatoes, peeled and sliced
½ pound apples, peeled, cored and sliced

1 In a large skillet, sauté onions in 1 tablespoon of the fat or oil. Remove onions from skillet and set aside.
2 Season liver with salt and pepper and cut into 1-inch slices. Heat remaining tablespoon of fat or oil in skillet, add liver and cook 2 minutes. Shake pan frequently to prevent burning.
3 Add broth, potatoes, apples and sautéed onions. Reduce heat, cover and simmer 30 minutes.
Serves 6

* To make liver Kosher, salt and broil a few minutes on each side in a preheated broiler. Rinse before using.

According to ancient precept in the Talmud, Adam and ten generations of his descendants were forbidden to eat meat. Thus, we read in the Book of Genesis, Chapter 1, verse 29, "And God said, Behold I have given you every herb bearing seed... to you it shall be for meat." This did not refer to animals and fowl. However, when Noah in his righteousness saved every living being on earth, he and the generations after him were permitted to eat meat. So that, upon Noah's leaving the ark, we read in Genesis, Chapter 9, verse 2-3, "And the fear and the dread of you shall be upon every beast of the earth and upon every fowl of the air, upon all that moveth upon the earth, and upon all the fishes of the sea; into your hand are they delivered. Every moving thing that liveth shall be meat for you; even as the green herb have I given you all things."

meats

Beef lung

(lungen)

2 pounds beef lung
2 tablespoons oil
4 large carrots, peeled and sliced
2 large onions, chopped
2 parsley roots, peeled and sliced
½ teaspoon salt
¼ teaspoon pepper
2 cups cold water

1 Clean lung thoroughly and cut into cubes.
2 Heat oil in a large skillet and sauté carrots, onions and parsley roots until tender. Add lung, salt, pepper and water, bring to a boil and simmer covered, 1-1 ½ hours.
Add more water if necessary. Serve with boiled potatoes.
Serves 6-8

poultry

AL GALLO

poultry

Chicken with mushrooms
(hendel mit shvammen)

2 small broiler-fryers, cut into serving pieces
½ cup bread crumbs
1 teaspoon salt
½ teaspoon pepper
margarine or oil for sautéeing
3 parsley roots, peeled and sliced
2 carrots, peeled and sliced
½ pound fresh mushrooms, sliced
1 cup cold water or chicken broth

1 Dredge chicken parts in bread crumbs seasoned with salt and pepper. In a heavy skillet, heat margarine or oil and sauté chicken on both sides until golden. Drain on absorbent paper towels.
2 Add parsley roots and carrots to skillet and sauté for a few minutes. Add mushrooms and cook until golden, adding more margarine or oil if necessary. Return chicken to skillet, add water or broth, cover and simmer 1 hour. Serve with boiled rice.
Serves 8

Chicken with oranges
(hendel mit marantzen)

2 small broiler chickens, cut into serving pieces
2 teaspoons salt
1 teaspoon pepper
1 teaspoon ground ginger (optional)
3 tablespoons margarine or oil
3 large oranges, peeled and thinly sliced crosswise
2 tablespoons brown sugar

1 Rub chicken with salt, pepper and ginger.
2 Heat margarine or oil in large skillet and lightly brown chicken on all sides.
3 Arrange chicken pieces in a Dutch oven alternating with layers of orange slices and ending with a top layer of orange. Sprinkle with brown sugar, cover and simmer over a low flame 1 hour.
Serves 6

When a Jew returned home from a wedding, he was asked what the meal had been like. He replied, "If the soup had been as hot as the wine, and if the wine had been as old as the chicken, and if the chicken had been as fat as the bride — it would have been an excellent meal."

●●●●●●●●●●●●

There are more shochets than chickens.

●●●●●●●●●●●●

If you let the dog and the cat prepare the feast, there'll be nothing left for the guests.

●●●●●●●●●●●●

You won't get healthier by eating and you won't get wiser by reading.

●●●●●●●●●●●●

If you don't have a citron, you may make the blessing over a potato.

●●●

Chicken with rice

(hendel mit reiz)

5 tablespoons oil
2 small onions, chopped
2 small broiler-fryer chickens, cut into serving pieces
2 teaspoons paprika
1 teaspoon salt
1 teaspoon pepper
3 cups cold water
1 ½ cups uncooked rice

1 Heat half the oil in a large, oven-proof skillet and sauté onions until golden. Set onions aside.
2 Sprinkle chicken pieces with paprika, salt and pepper. Heat remaining oil in skillet and sauté chicken pieces on both sides until golden brown.
3 Preheat oven to medium (325°F.).
4 Add water, rice and sautéed onions to skillet, cover and bring to a boil. Reduce heat and simmer 15-20 minutes. Remove from heat, uncover and bake 30 minutes or until chicken is browned.
Serves 8

poultry

Husham, the classic fool of many stories in Jewish folklore, was once working as a servant in the home of the richest Jew in town.
One day, the lady of the house said to him, "Husham, go to the butcher's and buy me a nice chicken."

Husham took the money and went to the butcher's. He remembered that his mistress had wanted an exceptional chicken and so he took a good look at the chickens, felt them all over looking for the best one.

The butcher saw Husham fingering all his chickens, so he pulled one out and said, "Here, Husham, take this one, it's a beauty, all pure fat."
Now Husham thought to himself, if the butcher says his best chicken is pure fat, that must mean that fat is better than chicken. I'll go and buy some fat instead.

He left the butcher's and went into another shop to ask for fat.
"Here, you won't find any finer fat in the whole city. Look, it's as clear as oil!" said the shop-keeper.
Husham thought again: If he says his finest fat is as clear as oil, it must mean that oil is better than fat. I'll go and buy some oil.
So he went to another shop to ask for oil.
Here the shop-keeper said, "Here you are, Grade A oil — as clear and pure as

Chicken stuffed with prunes
(gefilte hendel mit getrukente floymen)

1 pound prunes
4-pound roasting chicken
2 teaspoons salt
½ teaspoon pepper
1 teaspoon sweet paprika

1 Soak prunes in water to cover ½ hour. Drain and reserve liquid.
2 Preheat oven to moderate (350°F.).
3 Wash chicken inside and out. Pat dry and cut away any loose fat from the cavity. Sprinkle cavity with 1 teaspoon salt. In a separate bowl, combine remaining salt with pepper and paprika and sprinkle on chicken.
4 Loosely fill chicken cavity with drained prunes and roast in oven for 45 minutes. Baste frequently with prune liquid. After 45 minutes, surround chicken with remaining prunes and roast an additional 45 minutes or until chicken is done.
Serves 6

Color plate facing page 64.

Tamar's chicken
(Tamar's hendel)

2 pounds chicken breasts, boned and skinned
2 tablespoons oil
2 medium onions, finely chopped
4 large carrots, peeled and coarsely grated
2 green peppers, thinly sliced
6 cups chicken stock
1 ½ cups raw rice
salt and pepper to taste

1 Shred chicken coarsely.
2 Heat oil in a heavy skillet or Dutch oven and sauté onions until golden. Add chicken, carrots, peppers and 2 cups of the stock. Bring to a boil, cover and simmer gently 30 minutes.
3 Add the remaining stock, rice and salt and pepper to taste and continue simmering, covered, 30 minutes.
Serves 6

Chicken giblet fricassee
(pippiklech, fliegelech, helzelech un layberlech)

water."
"Aha," thought Husham, "if he says his purest oil is as clear as water, it must mean that water is better than oil." So he went to the river, drew a bucket of water and took it home to his mistress.

●●●

6 chicken gizzards
6 chicken wings
2 stalks celery with leaves, chopped
2 sprigs parsley, chopped
2 sprigs fresh dill or 1 teaspoon dried dill weed
3 chicken livers, halved*
2 tablespoons chicken fat or oil
2 medium onions, quartered
1 large green pepper, diced
salt and pepper to taste
1 tablespoon flour
paprika
fresh parsley

1 Clean gizzards in boiling water and slice each into 3 pieces. Place in saucepan with wings, celery, parsley and dill. Add cold water to cover, bring to a boil and simmer, covered, 1 hour. Add livers and simmer 15 minutes longer.
2 In a large skillet, heat fat or oil and sauté onions until transparent. Add green pepper and cook 10 minutes longer.
3 Remove gizzards, wings and livers from broth and add to onion-pepper mixture. Season with salt and pepper. Reserve the broth.
4 Sprinkle mixture with flour and continue cooking, stirring gently until vegetables and chicken are well coated. Stir in ½ cup of the broth and cook several minutes longer while sauce thickens. Sprinkle with paprika and garnish with parsley, if desired.
Note: The strained broth makes a very good soup.
Serves 6
* *To make chicken livers Kosher, salt and broil a few minutes on each side in a preheated broiler. Rinse before using.*

A man who was having a meal in a kosher restaurant called the waiter to complain.
"Waiter, the chicken you served was a very tough old bird!"
"How do you know, sir?"
"By the teeth."
"Teeth?" marveled the waiter. "Does a chicken have teeth?"
"No," retorted the guest, "but I have!"

A woman once went into a kosher butcher-shop and asked for a chicken. Although none of the chickens the butcher showed her met with her approval, she finally picked one out and began poking and pawing at its drumsticks, ribs, wings and the neck.
"Madam," said the butcher angrily, "if someone were to examine you in the same way, do you believe you'd pass the test?"

It's good to get close to a pot of schmaltz, for some of it is sure to rub off.

Chicken fat and cracklings
(schmaltz un grieben)

fat and fatty skin of 1 stewing chicken
salt to taste
1 large onion, chopped

1 Cut fat and fatty skin from chicken into small pieces, sprinkle with salt and place in heavy skillet. Cook, uncovered, on low flame, stirring often, until skin is brown, about 10 minutes. Add onions and sauté until golden brown.

2 Continue cooking until cracklings (grieben) are brown and crunchy, about 10-15 minutes. Turn off heat and remove onions and grieben with a slotted spoon. Store in a jar and refrigerate.

3 Strain and cool remaining chicken fat (schmaltz) before refrigerating in a separate jar.
Note: Goose cracklings and fat may also be prepared in this manner.

Chicken stuffed with prunes (page 62) accompanied by boiled potatoes sprinkled with parsley and Glazed carrots in honey (page 85) make a delicious meal.

How to make schmaltz and grieben

1 - 2 *Cut fatty skin from chicken and sprinkle with salt.*
  3 *Cook in hot skillet until brown.*
  4 *Add coarsely chopped onions and cook until golden.*
  5 *With a slotted spoon, remove onions and cracklings (grieben)
      when brown and crunchy.*
  6 *Pour remaining fat (schmaltz) into a jar.*

*Veal breast with kasha stuffing (page 56) is a tasty and interesting
combination.*

poultry

None ever kept the tradition of sending Purim gifts as much as the Jews of Chelm. As the Book of Esther says, Purim is "a day of gladness and feasting; a good day, a day of sending portions to one another." The Chelmans spared no pain in making their gifts attractive, using cookies of all shapes and colors and expensive fruits. In the gifts sent to the important people and to the Rabbi, they added the crowning glory — an orange!

For years, everything went well, but suddenly, the messengers began to steal the most attractive items and that year, the Rav did not taste an orange.

As next Purim approached, the Council of the Wise Men of Chelm met to discuss this problem. For seven days and nights they talked and talked. Finally, they decided to send their Purim gifts by messengers without hands so they would not be able to dip into the sacks containing the gifts. This failed because the handless messengers joined forces with the town hoodlums who stole the oranges and shared them with the messengers. And so, the Rav did not taste an orange that year.
The next year, the Council again sat for seven days and nights and decided to send messengers without hands

Stuffed chick neck
(gefilte helzel)

2 onions, chopped
⅓ cup goose or chicken fat
1 cup flour
salt, pepper and paprika to taste
skin of one whole chicken neck

1 Sauté onions in fat until translucent. Stir in flour, salt, pepper and paprika.
2 Wash and clean chicken neck in hot water. Pat dry inside and out. Sew up one end with heavy thread and stuff with onion-flour mixture. Sew up other end.
3 Set oven to slow (325°F.). Place stuffed neck in roasting pan and surround with any remaining stuffing. Roast 1½ hours, raise temperature to 350°F. and roast an additional ½-1 hour until skin is golden brown. Baste with drippings every ½ hour.
Serves 4

Poultry stuffing
(gefilechtz far a hendel)

½ loaf stale white bread, sliced
1 tablespoon oil or margarine
2 small onions, chopped
1 cup chopped fresh parsley
¼ cup finely chopped celery
1 egg, beaten
1 teaspoon salt
½ teaspoon sugar
dash of pepper

1 Soak bread in cold water to cover 5 minutes. Squeeze out water until almost dry.
2 Heat oil or margarine in a small skillet and sauté onions until transparent. Transfer to a bowl and add rest of ingredients. Mix lightly until mixture is blended.
3 Fill chicken cavity with stuffing or fill between skin and meat by following illustrated instructions on page 165.
Makes enough stuffing for 2 chickens

who were also dumb. But alas, this too failed as the messengers communicated with the hoodlums by sign language. Once again, they stole the most expensive things and once again the Rav did not taste an orange.

So, the following year, the Council met again for seven days and nights and decided to employ messengers without hands who could neither talk nor see. But even that didn't help for the messengers took the packages home where their wives and children took the best things out and once again the Rav did not have an orange.

The next year, the Council was in despair. After seven days and nights they finally decided that from that time on, Purim gifts would be sent by messengers who had no hands, who could not speak, who could not see and who could not walk. Therefore, the original senders would have to carry the messengers on their backs to deliver the gifts.

That year, for the first time in ages, Purim was truly a happy festival in Chelm. At long last, the Rav got to taste an orange and all the messengers earned a handsome fee for there were only a few in Chelm without hands and legs who could neither see nor talk.

● ● ●

Turkey schnitzel
(indik shnitzel)

2 pounds turkey breasts, sliced ½-inch thick
prepared mustard
1 egg, beaten
½ cup seasoned bread crumbs
3 tablespoons oil
lemon slices, halved

1 Pound turkey slices lightly until thin. Spread a thin layer of mustard on each slice. Dip in egg and dredge in bread crumbs.
2 Heat oil in skillet and sauté schnitzels 4-5 minutes on each side. Serve at once garnished with lemon slices accompanied by Buckwheat with noodles (page 81).
Note: Chicken breasts may also be prepared in the same way, but reduce sautéeing time to 2-3 minutes on each side.
Serves 6

poultry

Roast goose with potato stuffing
(gebrotene ganz mit kartoffel gefilechtz)

8-pound goose
5 large potatoes, boiled, peeled and mashed
½ cup minced parsley
½ cup grated onion
1 egg, beaten
1 teaspoon caraway seeds
salt and pepper to taste

1 Preheat oven to moderate (350°F.).
2 Pat the goose dry with a damp cloth inside and out.
3 Combine the mashed potatoes with all the remaining
  ingredients and stuff the goose loosely. Truss the goose and
  place it, breast up, on a rack in an open roasting pan. Prick
  the skin. Roast about 3 hours (20-25 minutes per pound of
  goose), basting often and pricking the skin occasionally.
  Goose is done when the leg joints move readily.
Serves 8

Roast duck with apples and pears
(gebrotene katshke mit eppel un barness)

4-pound duckling
1 teaspoon salt
½ teaspoon pepper
2 onions, chopped
2 large cooking apples, peeled, cored and quartered
2 large firm pears, peeled, cored and quartered

1 Preheat oven to moderate (350°F.).
2 Wash duck and pat dry inside and out. Rub skin and cavity
  with salt and pepper.
3 Place duck in roasting pan, sprinkle inside and out with
  onions and surround with fruit. Roast 1½ hours, basting
  duck and fruit occasionally with drippings. Serve with hot
  boiled rice.
Serves 8

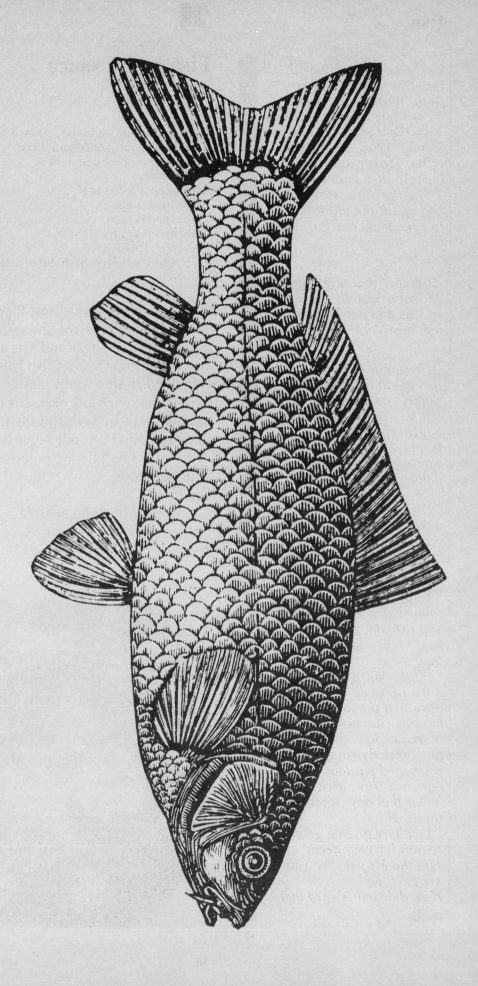

fish

fish

There was once a Jewish tailor in Rome who went to the market on the eve of Yom Kippur to buy a fish. Now there was only one fish left which the servant of the Mayor wanted to buy. So they both bid for it and the price went up and up till the tailor bid twelve dinars and got the fish.

At dinner that night, the Mayor asked his servant why he had not brought him any fish.

"There was only one fish for sale in the market today," answered the fellow, "and some Jew bought it for a dinar a pound. You wouldn't have wanted me to pay twelve dinars for a fish, would you?"
"Do you know this Jew?" asked his master.
"Yes, I do," said the servant.

The Mayor sent for the tailor and asked, "How do you explain, Jew, that you paid twelve dinars for a fish?"
"With your permission, my lord, I will explain," answered the tailor, "We have one day which is more precious to us than any other day in the year, when God pardons us for our sins. Now, aren't we to honor that day, whatever the cost?"
"You have given a good reason for your deed," said the Mayor, "so you are excused."
How did God reward that

➡

Fish in dill sauce
(fish in kriep-sohs)

2 pounds carp or white fish, cleaned,* with head
1 medium carrot, peeled and sliced
1 parsley root, peeled and sliced
pinch of sugar
salt and pepper to taste
2 tablespoons butter
2 tablespoons flour
2 tablespoons sour cream
1 teaspoon lemon juice
3 tablespoons minced fresh dill or 1 tablespoon dried dill weed

1 Slice fish into 1-inch slices. Place slices and head in 3-quart soup kettle with carrot and parsley root. Add water to cover and sprinkle in sugar and salt and pepper. Bring to a boil, cover and simmer until fish is tender, about 30 minutes. Remove fish to a warm platter, strain and reserve broth.
2 Melt butter over low heat, stir in flour thoroughly, and gradually stir in 2 cups of the fish broth, sour cream, lemon juice and dill. Pour dill sauce over fish, or serve alongside. Serve with small boiled potatoes or with hot noodles mixed with the sauce.

Serves 4
* See illustrations on page 73.

tailor? He found a fine
pearl inside the fish, which
provided him with a living
for the rest of his life.

●●●●●●●●●●●

"I'm afraid this fish must
be from last year," said
the man to the waiter.
"How should I know?"
returned the waiter, "I've
only been working here for
six weeks. . ."

●●●

Fish baked in sour cream
(fish gebroten in smetene)

2 pounds carp or pike, cleaned* and cut
in 1-inch pieces or 6 whole small carp or pike, cleaned
1 teaspoon salt
½ teaspoon pepper
2 large onions sliced
1 cup sour cream
1 tablespoon paprika
2 tablespoons melted butter

1 Preheat oven to slow (325°F.).
2 Arrange fish in greased baking dish, sprinkle with salt and
pepper and top with onions.
3 Mix sour cream with paprika and pour over the fish. Bake 45
minutes, basting frequently with the melted butter.
Serves 6
See illustrations on page 73.

Baked mackerel
(gebrotene makerel)

2 onions, sliced
1 large, firm tomato, sliced
2 medium potatoes, peeled and thinly sliced
3 stalks celery, diced
2 pounds mackerel fillets*
juice of 1 lemon
salt and pepper to taste
2 tablespoons butter or margarine
paprika

1 Preheat oven to moderate (350°F.).
2 Arrange half the vegetables on the bottom of a buttered
baking dish. Add fillets, sprinkle with lemon juice and salt
and pepper to taste and dot with butter or margarine.
3 Cover fish with remaining vegetables and sprinkle with
paprika. Cover with lid or tinfoil and bake about 30 minutes,
or until fish flakes easily with a fork.
Serves 4
* Any white fish may be substituted.
Color plate facing page 80.

71

There were always some
Hassidim who liked to
recount tales of wonder
and miracles,
exaggerating more than a
little. One day, two such
Hassidim were chatting
and one of them said,
"Once, when I was visiting
my Rabbi, I saw them
bring a fish to his house
which was fifteen meters
long!"
"I was once in the
market," said the other,
"and saw them selling
gigantic pots, each as high
as the tower in the town
hall."
"What would you need
such big pots for?" asked
the first.
"To cook your Rabbi's
fish in, of course!" came
the retort.

●●●●●●●●●●●

A man once went into
a kosher restaurant and
ordered fish, but when his
order was brought, the fish
was not fresh. He bent
over and began to whisper
to the fish. The owner
went over to him and
asked, "May I ask what
you are doing, sir?"
"I'm having a chat with
the fish," he replied. "I
asked where it came from
and it said — from the
River Danube, so I asked
for news of the Danube.
Do you know what it
answered? 'How should I
know? I left over a month
ago. . .'"

●●●

Fish baked in tomato sauce
(fish gebroten in tomatten-sohs)

2 pounds carp or pike, cleaned and cut into 1-inch pieces
1 teaspoon salt
½ teaspoon pepper
1 tablespoon fresh chopped, parsley
2 tablespoons oil
3 medium onions, thinly sliced
1 small green pepper, cleaned and chopped
1 cup tomato paste
1 cup cold water
1 teaspoon dried oregano
½ teaspoon ground nutmeg

1 Preheat oven to moderate (350°F.).
2 Rub fish with salt and pepper, sprinkle with parsley and arrange in greased baking dish. Set aside.
3 In a small saucepan, heat oil and sauté onions and green pepper. Sprinkle over fish.
4 Dilute tomato paste with the water, stir in oregano and nutmeg and pour over fish. Bake 35-45 minutes, basting occasionally.
Serves 6

How to clean a fish

1 *Rinse fish in cold water. While still wet, scrape scales from tail to head with the dull edge of a knife.*
2 *Cut off fins and tail.*
3 *With the sharp blade of a knife pointing outwards, slit the underside of fish from belly to head.*
4 *Remove and discard entrails.*
5 *Press out gills underneath head with fingers.*
6 *Thoroughly rinse inside and out in cold running water.*

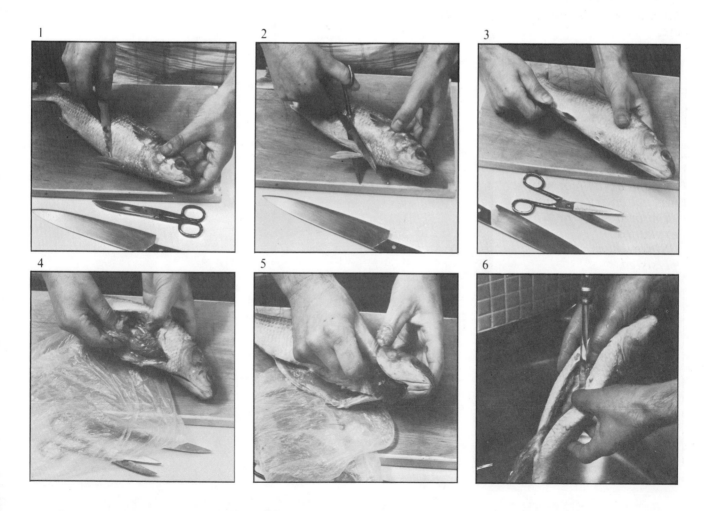

fish

Moses Mendelssohn, the famous philosopher, was once invited to a banquet at the home of an important German baron. During the meal Mendelssohn ate only the kosher dishes which had been specially prepared for him. The archbishop who was seated next to him, looked on with a mocking smile and asked, "When will you finally allow yourself to eat our food, Sir?" Mendelssohn smiled and replied, "At your wedding, my Lord!"

●●●●●●●●●●●●

Rabbi Meyer loved fish, but he only ate fish from Sunday until Wednesday, so that he could enjoy them anew on Shabbat eve.

●●●●●●●●●●●●

The Jewish humorist Sami Groenemann was once at a banquet of German writers and since the food was not kosher, he abstained from eating. His friends noticed this and asked him why he was not eating anything. "I'm on a diet," he explained. "Since when?" they persisted. "Since 2000 years ago," Groenemann replied.

●●●●●●●●●●●●

Fish and guests begin to smell bad on the third day.

●●●

Baked herring with sour cream
(gebakene herring)

3 schmaltz herrings cleaned
2 cups thinly sliced onion rings
boiling water
3 tablespoons butter
2/3 cup sour cream

1 The night before, soak herrings in water to cover. Change water frequently.

2 The next day, place onion rings in a small saucepan, cover with boiling water and bring to a boil again. Remove from heat and drain.

3 Preheat oven to moderate (350°F.).

4 Remove herrings from water, rinse and fillet (see illustrations on page 19). Cut into serving pieces and place in small, greased casserole dish.

5 Add boiled onion rings to casserole dish, dot with butter and bake until onions are browned, about 40-45 minutes. Add sour cream and bake 10 minutes longer.

Serves 4-6

Baked herring with apples and potatoes
(gebrotene herring)

3 salt herrings
2 slices white bread
½ cup milk
1 medium onion, chopped
butter
2 eggs, beaten
1 large cooking apple, peeled and grated
2 potatoes, boiled, peeled and mashed
salt and pepper to taste
bread crumbs

1 Soak herrings in water to cover overnight, changing water
  frequently.
2 Preheat oven to moderate (350°F.).
3 Fillet herring by splitting down center and carefully removing
  backbone and small bones (see illustrations on page 19).
4 Soak bread slices in milk until absorbed. Sauté onions in
  butter until golden.
5 Arrange herring fillets in a greased baking dish. Pour beaten
  eggs over and cover with bread slices, onions, grated apple
  and mashed potatoes seasoned with salt and pepper. Toss
  bread crumbs in melted butter and sprinkle on top. Bake 30-
  40 minutes or until crust is lightly browned.
Serves 4

Rabbi Abraham Joshua Heshel used to say, "If I had my way, I would abolish all fast days except two — Yom Kippur and Tisha b'Av. For who needs to eat on Yom Kippur, which is the Day of Judgment? And who can eat on Tisha b'Av which commemorates the destruction of the Temple?"

●●●

Russian fish stew
(russishe fish eingekochtz)

2 pounds fresh carp or pike, cleaned*
juice of 1 lemon
1 tablespoon butter or margarine
2 large onions, sliced
2 carrots, peeled and sliced
1 medium parsley root, peeled
6 medium potatoes, peeled and thickly sliced
2 bay leaves
1 teaspoon salt
freshly ground pepper to taste

1 Cut fish into 1-inch slices, sprinkle with lemon juice and refrigerate 6 hours or overnight.
2 Melt fat in a large skillet and sauté onions, carrots and parsley root until tender.
3 Add remaining ingredients to skillet with cold water to cover, bring to a boil and simmer, covered, 1 hour. Before serving remove bay leaves and parsley root, if desired.
Serves 4
* See illustrations on page 73.

pastas and cereals

The tavern keeper likes the drunk but he will never let him marry his daughter.

Eating together with your relatives you can, but never from the same plate.

Food gives you an appetite, but an appetite doesn't give you food.

God created food as the devil delicacies.

Don't eat much, but eat all the time.

You have a little hole in your throat, that swallows all your money.

You forget all your troubles in the joy of success.

Hunger is the best spice of all.

Apple, cheese and noodle pudding
(lokshen kugel mit kayz un eppel)

1 pound broad noodles
boiling salted water
4 tablespoons melted butter or margarine
4 eggs, slightly beaten
½ cup sugar
1 cup cream cheese
1 cup cottage cheese
½ pint sour cream
5 green apples, peeled, cored and chopped
½ cup seedless raisins

1 Preheat oven to moderate (350°F.).
2 Cook noodles according to package directions until tender but firm. Drain and put in deep mixing bowl.
3 Pour melted fat over noodles. Add remaining ingredients and mix well. Turn mixture into large, well-greased baking dish and bake 1 hour or until crust is golden brown.
Variation: Traditionally, dried apples were used instead of fresh apples. If desired, soak ¾ cup dried apples in water to cover ½ hour, drain, chop coarsely and proceed as directed.
Serves 6-8
Color plate facing page 81.

Baked noodles with cheese
(lokshen un kayz kugel)

1 pound broad noodles
4 tablespoons butter
4 eggs, separated
⅓ cup sugar
½ teaspoon cinnamon
pinch of salt
2 cups creamed cottage cheese
½ cup cream cheese, softened
1 cup seedless raisins

1 Preheat oven to moderate (350°F.).
2 Cook noodles according to package directions until almost tender. Drain and place in large mixing bowl. Add butter and mix until melted.
3 Beat egg yolks with sugar, cinnamon and salt, stir in cottage cheese and cream cheese and mix in the raisins. Combine with noodles.
4 Beat egg whites until stiff and fold into noodle mixture. Pour into greased baking dish and bake 35 minutes. Raise heat to 400°F. and bake an additional 10 minutes so that crust is golden brown.
Serves 8

A good Jewish housewife is always prepared for the unexpected guest. Smaller slices in the kugel, *an extra cup of water in the soup and the meal is ready!*

Because the milkman used to water down his milk, his customers would say: You only get pure milk from the cow.

Who is a good housewife? The woman who gives everyone his share, but leaves something for herself too.

If you can't eat what you like, you'd better like what you eat.

Better put it in your mouth than take it to your heart!

Plump cheeks show what the teeth chew.

Baked noodles with raisins and nuts
(lokshen kugel)

½ pound broad noodles
2 eggs, separated
½ cup sugar
¼ teaspoon cinnamon
¼ teaspoon nutmeg
1/8 teaspoon salt
3 tablespoons butter or margarine
½ cup raisins or ½ cup peeled, cored and chopped apples
¼ cup chopped walnuts
butter or margarine for topping
3 tablespoons bread crumbs

1 Preheat oven to hot (400°F.).
2 Cook noodles according to package directions until tender. Drain.
3 Beat egg yolks with sugar, cinnamon, nutmeg and salt. Add drained noodles, butter or margarine, raisins or chopped apples and walnuts and mix well.
4 Beat egg whites until stiff and gently fold into noodle mixture. Pour into greased casserole dish, dot with butter or margarine and cover with bread crumbs. Bake 45 minutes.
Serves 4

Baked noodles

(lokshen kugel)

½ pound broad egg noodles
3 eggs, separated
3 tablespoons melted chicken fat or margarine
2 tablespoons sugar
½ teaspoon salt

1 Preheat oven to moderate (350°F.).
2 Cook noodles according to package directions until tender. Drain and place in mixing bowl.
3 Beat egg yolks and add fat, sugar and salt. Beat again until mixture is smooth. Fold egg mixture into noodles.
4 Beat egg whites until stiff. Gently fold into noodle mixture.
5 Transfer to deep, greased baking dish, even out surface and bake 30-40 minutes or until brown on top.
Serves 4

Baked mackerel (page 71) makes a hearty main dish.

Rabbi Pinchas, the Tzaddik of Koritz, used to say that Jews eat lots of lokshen *on Shabbat because noodles are symbolic of the unity of the People of Israel: They are so entangled that they can never be separated.*

If she can't make a kugel—divorce her!

Everyone has a good appetite at a feast prepared by someone else.

A man once ordered lokshen *in a restaurant, tasted them and called to the waiter to bring him some vinegar.*
"Vinegar," asked the waiter, "what for?"
"This sauerkraut you've served me," said the man, "isn't sour enough."
"I didn't serve you sauerkraut," the waiter said, "that is lokshen.*"*
"Oh," said the man, "if this is lokshen, *then they are much too sour."*

In Yiddish, porridge is called kashe *and pronounced just like the Hebrew word* kushiyah *which means a problem and is used a great deal in the study of Talmud.*

They say that when Rabbi Abraham Joshua Heshel was a bright little boy, he was once eating kashe *when his father asked him with a smile, "Heshele, can you explain this* kashe?"

"Our sages tell us," said the boy, "not to talk when we are eating, so I can't answer you now."

His father waited till he had finished and repeated his question. "Can you explain the kashe *now?"*

The boy answered quickly, "There is no kashe *now!"*

● ● ●

Buckwheat with noodles

(gretchene kashe mit lokshen)

1 cup buckwheat (kasha)
2 egg yolks, beaten
1 teaspoon salt
2½ cups boiling water
1 tablespoon oil
1 onion, minced
1 cup bow tie noodles
4 tablespoons oil

1 Brown the kasha in a large, hot skillet, stirring constantly to avoid burning. Quickly stir in the egg yolks to prevent them from setting and continue stirring until the grains are fully coated. Add salt and water, reduce heat and cook until grains are tender, about 8 minutes.

2 Meanwhile, heat the oil in a small skillet and sauté onions until golden.

3 Preheat oven to hot (400°F).

4 Cook noodles according to package directions until tender. Drain.

5 In a 2-quart casserole dish, combine kasha, onions and noodles. Dot with butter or oil and bake 12-15 minutes.

Serves 6-8

81

Shavuoth is the time for dairy dishes. Pictured clockwise: Shavuoth cheesecake (page 142), Mushrooms with sour cream (page 86) and Apple and noodle cheese pudding (page 78).

Buckwheat with onions
(gretchene kashe mit tzibbeles)

1 cup buckwheat (kasha)
1 egg, lightly beaten
1 cup boiling water
1 teaspoon salt
¼ cup chicken fat or oil
2 onions, diced
1 cup beef bouillon

1 Brown kasha in hot skillet and cook over high heat until kasha is toasted, stirring constantly to avoid burning, about 3-5 minutes. Stir in beaten egg and cook 5 minutes, stirring until all the grains are coated. Add boiling water and salt, cover and cook over medium flame until kasha is tender, about 15 minutes.

2 In a separate large skillet, heat fat or oil and sauté onions until golden brown.

3 Drain any excess water from kasha, add to onions and mix well. Add bouillon and cook, uncovered, over a high flame until bouillon is reduced but kasha is still slightly moist, about 10 minutes.

Serves 4-6

vegetables

Red cabbage and apples
(roit-kroit mit eppel)

1 medium red cabbage, shredded
boiling water
3 tablespoons margarine
1 small onion, chopped
½ pound tart cooking apples, peeled, cored and sliced
1 tablespoon sugar
2 teaspoons caraway seeds
1 teaspoon paprika
1 teaspoon salt

1 Place shredded cabbage in a deep bowl and scald with boiling water to cover. Let stand 10 minutes. Drain.
2 Heat margarine in large skillet and sauté onions until golden. Add apples along with remaining ingredients to skillet, cover and cook over a low flame 1 hour or until cabbage is soft. Add water if necessary to keep mixture moist. Serve immediately.
Serves 6

Red cabbage in wine
(roit-kroit in vein)

2 tablespoons margarine
1 medium onion, finely chopped
1 large red cabbage, finely shredded
1 large cooking apple, peeled and coarsely grated
½ cup dry red wine
¼ cup cider vinegar
2 tablespoons sugar
1 teaspoon salt

1 Melt margarine in a saucepan and sauté onions until golden.
2 Add rest of ingredients, bring to a boil and simmer 30 minutes, stirring occasionally. Serve either hot or cold. Goes especially well with a meat entrée.
Serves 6-8
Color plate facing page 33.

Glazed carrots in honey
(mayeren glentzedige in honig)

1 pound carrots, peeled and sliced
boiling salted water
1 tablespoon corn flour
1 ½ teaspoons honey
1 ½ teaspoons sugar
2 tablespoons margarine

1 Cook sliced carrots in boiling salted water to cover until partially tender, 5-10 minutes. Reserve ½ cup of the carrot liquid and drain the carrots.
2 Mix the corn flour with carrot liquid and combine with honey and sugar. Melt margarine in a skillet, add carrots, stir in corn flour - honey mixture and continue stirring until carrots are well coated. Cook over a low flame until carrots are glazed and tender, about 5 minutes.
Serves 6
Color plate facing page 64.

Okra with corn and green peppers
(okra mit korn-kerndlech un griene feffers)

1 pound okra
2 tablespoons margarine
1 medium onion, chopped
2 green peppers, chopped
3 ounces tomato paste
½ cup cold water
2 teaspoons brown sugar
1 teaspoon sugar
1 teaspoon salt
½ teaspoon paprika
¼ teaspoon curry powder
1 cup canned corn, drained

1 Wash the okra and cut off stems. Slice the pods.
2 Melt fat in a large skillet and sauté okra, onions and peppers. Add remaining ingredients, cover and simmer until vegetables are tender, about 5 minutes, stirring a few times.
Serves 4

Sautéed cauliflower florets
(gepregelte kalifior)

2-pound head of cauliflower
cold salted water
1 egg, beaten
¾ cup seasoned bread crumbs
½ cup butter or margarine

1 Place cauliflower in a saucepan with cold salted water and bring to a boil. Cover, reduce heat and simmer until barely tender. Drain and separate the stalks from the florets.
2 Dip florets in egg and dredge in bread crumbs. Melt butter or margarine in a skillet and sauté florets until golden brown, about 10 minutes.
Serves 4

Mushrooms with sour cream
(shvammen mit smetene)

1 pound fresh mushrooms, thinly sliced
1 small onion, chopped
2 tablespoons butter
salt and pepper to taste
2 teaspoons flour
1 cup sour cream, room temperature

1 Sauté mushrooms and onions in butter until tender. Season with salt and pepper to taste, mix in flour, cover, reduce heat and continue to cook 5 minutes.
2 Remove to serving dish and gradually stir in sour cream a little at a time. Serve at once.
Serves 4
Color plate facing page 81.

Baked peppers with egg
(gebakene feffers mit ayer)

4 large green peppers
boiling water
8 eggs
1 tablespoon chopped parsley
salt and pepper to taste

1 Preheat oven to moderate (350°F.).
2 Cut the peppers in half lengthwise and remove seeds and
  pith. Parboil in boiling water to cover 3-5 minutes. Drain.
3 Arrange the peppers in a greased shallow baking pan.
  Carefully break 1 egg into each half, keeping yolks intact.
  Sprinkle with parsley and salt and pepper and bake 15-20
  minutes or until peppers are tender.
Serves 8

vegetables

You must get so drunk on Purim that you can't tell the difference between "cursed be Haman" and "blessed be Mordecai," exhorts the Talmud, and various interpretations have been given to this counsel.

One commentator says that the Talmud does not say that you have to get drunk on wine but that you have to be as merry and carefree as if you had drunk lots of wine.

Another contends that every Jew knows very well that we are still slaves to various Ahasueruses and persecuted by Hamans, so unless he first gets drunk, how can he forget his troubles and enjoy Purim properly?

We find yet another interpretation in the book, Talks of the Sages. *The miserly rich, it says, are somewhat put out on Purim, because they must spend money on gifts for the poor, which is why they curse Haman, for he was the cause of it all. On the other hand, the poor rejoice on Purim because they receive lots of gifts and money — which is why they bless Mordecai who introduced this custom. Among Yemenite Jews it was the custom on Purim not to say "Lehayim" when they drank wine, but one would say "Cursed be Haman!" and the other would answer, "Blessed be*

Stuffed peppers I
(gefilte feffers I)

6 large peppers
1 ½ cups cottage cheese (12 ounces)
½ cup fresh chopped parsley
½ cup finely chopped chives or scallions
2 eggs, beaten
salt to taste

1 Preheat oven to moderate (350°F.).
2 Slice off tops of peppers, place in saucepan with cold water and boil 5 minutes. Drain and remove seeds and pith.
3 Mix remaining ingredients together and stuff peppers with the mixture.
4 Arrange peppers in a shallow baking dish, add just enough water to cover bottom of dish and bake 30 minutes or until peppers are tender.
Note: Jews have a special claim to scallions ("eshaklon" in Hebrew), which were discovered by the Crusaders in Ashkelon.
Serves 6

Stuffed peppers II
(gefilte feffers II)

6 large green peppers
2 medium tomatoes
1 cup rice
2 ½ cups salted boiling water
2 teaspoons butter or oil
2 onions, chopped
½ teaspoon dried basil
salt and pepper to taste
½ cup grated cheese

1 Preheat oven to moderate (350°F.).
2 Slice off tops of peppers and remove pith and seeds. Pour boiling water over and steep 3-5 minutes. Drain and set aside.
3 Blanch tomatoes by pouring boiling water over them. Let stand 5 minutes, peel and chop. Set aside.
4 Cook rice in the boiling salted water until partially tender but still firm, about 10 minutes. Drain
5 Heat butter or oil in a medium skillet and sauté onions until transparent. Stir in tomatoes, rice and seasonings and cook 3-5 minutes. Correct seasonings if necessary. Stuff peppers with the mixture and sprinkle with grated cheese.
6 Arrange stuffed peppers in a shallow baking dish, adding water to barely cover the bottom. Bake 40 minutes or until tender.
Serves 6

When boys of poor families left home to study at a Yeshiva in Eastern Europe, they used to eat at the homes of rich Jews who took it upon themselves to feed the students. Each Yeshiva-bocher *would have regular "days" — he would take his meal in a different home each day of the week. There were always some families who were generous, but there were also some who did their good deed grudgingly.*

Now there was one such stingy man who regularly gave his student only boiled potatoes, which were very cheap. When he was thoroughly fed up with this, the Yeshiva-bocher *one day turned to his host and asked, "What's the blessing we have to make on potatoes?"*

"You ignoramus!" cried his host, "Don't you know that we say 'Blessed art Thou, O Lord our God, King of the Universe, who brings forth the fruit of the earth' for all kinds of vegetables that come out of the ground?"
"Of course, I do,"retorted the student, "but which blessing do we say when they start coming out of your ears!"

Potato bake
(totsh)

1 tablespoon oil
3 medium onions, diced
5 medium potatoes, peeled
boiling salted water
3 eggs, separated
salt and pepper to taste

1 In a small skillet, heat oil and sauté onions until lightly browned.
2 Cook potatoes in the boiling salted water until tender. Drain and mash well.
3 Preheat oven to hot (400°F.).
4 Beat egg yolks until foamy, add to mashed potatoes and beat until creamy. Add onions and mix well.
5 Beat egg whites until stiff and gently fold into potato mixture. Add salt and pepper to taste. Turn mixture into well-greased baking dish and bake 45 minutes or until crust is golden brown.
Serves 6
Color plate facing page 128.

Potato pudding I
(kartoffel kugel I)

6 large potatoes, peeled and quartered
3 medium onions, peeled and chopped
¼ cup butter or margarine
2 eggs, beaten
3 tablespoons flour
1 teaspoon baking powder
salt to taste
dash of pepper
dash of ground nutmeg

1 Preheat oven to hot (400°F.).
2 Cook potatoes in water to cover until soft. Drain and mash.
3 Sauté onions in fat. Pour over potatoes, mix in remaining ingredients, put in greased casserole dish and bake 45 minutes or until *kugel* has a golden crust.
Serves 6-8

Sautéed potatoes with onions
(gepregelte kartoffel-plitshen mit tzibbeles)

5 tablespoons margarine
2 medium onions, chopped
2 pounds potatoes, peeled and thinly sliced
salt and pepper to taste

1 Melt 2 tablespoons of the fat in a large skillet and sauté the onions until golden. Set onions aside.
2 Melt remaining fat in the skillet, add potatoes and cook over a low flame, covered tightly, until tender, about 35 minutes.
3 Add onions and salt and pepper and continue cooking over a low flame until potatoes are golden brown, about 10 minutes.
Serves 4-6

Baked spinach with cream cheese
(gebakene shpinat mit fett-kayz)

2 pounds fresh spinach
boiling salted water
8 ounces cream cheese, softened
2 eggs, beaten
2 tablespoons matzo meal
dash of ground nutmeg
butter

1 Preheat oven to moderate (350° F.).
2 Wash spinach leaves thoroughly, discarding wilted leaves and longer stems. Chop spinach and cook in covered saucepan with a small amount of boiling salted water 10-15 minutes. Drain.
3 Mix spinach with cream cheese, eggs, matzo meal and nutmeg. Transfer to a baking dish greased with butter and bake 20 minutes. Top should be crusty.
Serves 6

No one knows exactly how the name kugel *came into use. One of the versions is that* kugel *is a reminder of the manna that the Children of Israel ate in the wilderness when they came out of Egypt. Rashi, the famous Jewish commentator on the Bible, claims that the seed of manna was round. Others contend that the word comes from the Hebrew* kugel — *like a disc — so that in form it resembles the manna that our forefathers ate in the desert.*

If you eat kugel *on the Sabbath, you'll be full the whole week.*

vegetables

●●●

Mixed vegetable croquettes
(gemieze latkelech)

2 zucchini, cubed
1 large eggplant, peeled and cubed
2 large carrots, peeled and sliced
2 large tomatoes, quartered
boiling salted water
1 egg, beaten
4 tablespoons matzo meal
½ teaspoon salt
¼ teaspoon pepper
dash of grated nutmeg
oil for frying

1 Place vegetables in a pot with a small amount of boiling salted water. Cover pot and simmer until vegetables are tender. Drain vegetables very well, mash and cool.
2 Mix mashed vegetables with egg, matzo meal and seasonings. With wet hands, form into 3-inch patties.
3 Heat a small amount of oil in a large skillet until very hot and fry a few croquettes at a time until brown on both sides. Drain on absorbent paper. May be topped with a dollop of sour cream.
Serves 6

Sauteed zucchini with tomatoes
(gepregelte bastaniklech mit tomatten)

½ cup minced onions
1 tablespoon margarine
½ pound zucchini, cubed
½ pound tomatoes, cubed
½ cup water
½ teaspoon salt
pinch of sugar

1 Sauté the onions in margarine until golden. Add zucchini, sauté 2 minutes, add tomatoes and sauté another 2 minutes.
2 Add water, salt and suger. Cover and simmer about 10 minutes, or until zucchini are tender but firm.
Serves 4-6

Stuffed zucchini
(gefilte bastaniklech)

6 zucchini
½ cup raw rice
1 ½ cups boiling salted water
½ cup cooked chicken, minced
½ cup salami, minced
1 egg, beaten
1 garlic clove, crushed
1 teaspoon oregano
salt and pepper to taste
1 tablespoon margarine or oil
2 medium onions, chopped
1 cup tomato sauce

1 Slice zucchini in half lengthwise and scoop out pulp. Chop pulp and reserve with zucchini shells.
2 Preheat oven to moderate (375°F.).
3 Cook rice in the boiling salted water until partially tender but still firm, about 10 minutes. Drain. Combine with zucchini pulp, chicken, salami, egg, garlic and seasonings.
4 Heat margarine or oil in a large skillet and sauté onions until tendér. Stir in zucchini mixture and simmer 3-5 minutes.
5 Stuff zucchini shells with the mixture and arrange in a baking pan. Add enough water to cover the bottom of the pan, spoon tomato sauce over stuffed zucchini and bake 30-40 minutes or until tender.
Serves 6

vegetables

Carrot and apple casserole
(gebakene mayeren un eppel tzimmes)

6 medium carrots, peeled and sliced
4 green apples, peeled, cored and sliced
1 tablespoon melted chicken fat or margarine
½ cup brown sugar
½ teaspoon cinnamon
dash of nutmeg
salt and pepper to taste

1 In a medium saucepan, simmer carrots in water to cover for 10 minutes. Add apples and simmer an additional 10 minutes. Drain.
2 Preheat oven to moderate (350°F.).
3 Liberally grease a casserole dish and add carrots and apples. Mix melted fat with brown sugar, cinnamon, nutmeg and salt and pepper. Sprinkle over carrots and apples and bake, covered, ½ hour. Remove cover and continue baking 15 minutes longer or until crust is well browned.
Serves 6

Lentils and salami
(linzen mit vursht)

1 pound dried lentils
1 tablespoon oil
2 medium onions, chopped
½ pound salami diced
salt and pepper to taste

1 The night before, rinse lentils several times until water is clear and drain. Place lentils in large saucepan, cover with cold water and soak overnight.
2 The next day, bring lentils and water to a boil, cover, reduce heat and simmer 30 minutes or until lentils are soft. Drain and set aside.
3 Heat oil in a large skillet and sauté onions until golden. Stir in salami and cook 5 minutes. Add lentils and salt and pepper to taste, stir and cook 5 minutes longer.
Serves 4-6

94

Stuffed peppers III
(gefilte feffers III)

6 large green peppers
½ cup raw rice
1 ½ cups boiling salted water
1 tablespoon oil
½ pound ground beef
3 ounces tomato paste diluted in ½ cup water
½ teaspoon garlic powder
salt and pepper to taste

1 Slice the tops off the peppers and remove seeds and pith. Reserve tops. Pour boiling water over peppers and steep 3-5 minutes. Drain and set aside.
2 Preheat oven to moderate (350°F.).
3 Cook the rice in boiling salted water until partially tender but still firm, about 10 minutes. Drain and set aside.
4 Heat the oil in a medium skillet and brown the meat.
5 Mix the rice, meat, tomato paste and seasonings. Stuff the peppers with the mixture. Cover with the tops.
6 Arrange peppers in a shallow baking dish, adding water to cover the bottom of the dish. Bake until peppers are tender, about 45 minutes - 1 hour, adding more water if necessary.
Serves 6

Potato casserole
(eingedempte kartoffel)

6 large potatoes, peeled and grated
1 medium onion, grated
½ cup chicken fat or oil
2 eggs, separated
½ cup flour
1 teaspoon baking powder
salt and pepper to taste
dash of grated nutmeg

1 Preheat oven to hot (400°F.).
2 Combine grated potatoes and onions. Drain off excess water. Mix with fat or oil. Beat egg yolks and add.
3 Sift together flour, baking powder and seasonings. Stir into potato mixture and blend well.
4 Beat egg whites until stiff and fold into potato mixture. Turn into square baking dish and bake 1 hour or until crust is golden brown.
Serves 6

Grated potato pudding II
(geribbene kartoffel kugel II)

6 large potatoes
1 medium onion
3 eggs, beaten
4 tablespoons chicken fat or margarine
1 teaspoon baking powder
salt to taste
dash of pepper

1 Preheat oven to hot (400°F.).
2 Peel and grate potatoes. Drain thoroughly. Grate and drain onion. Mix potatoes and onions with remaining ingredients.
3 Pour into a well-greased baking dish and bake 1 hour or until crust is brown. Garnish with applesauce or sugar.
Serves 6

eggs and salads

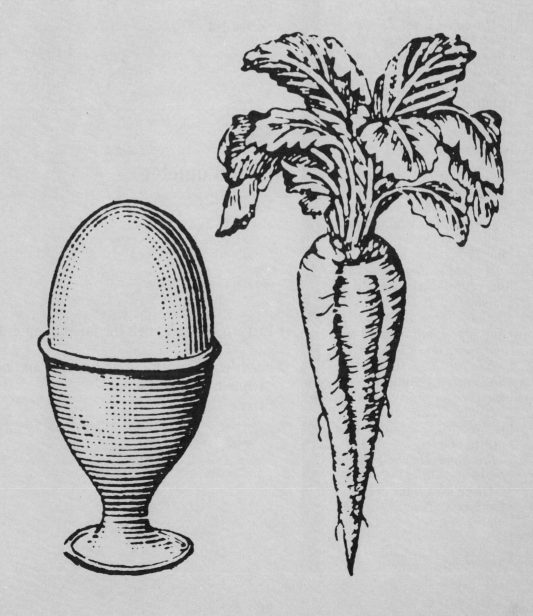

eggs and salads

The famous Yiddish writer, Shalom Aleichem tells about a poor man who visited the home of the G'vir (the richest Jew in the town) one morning and saw him eating an omelet. He went home and told his wife, "D'you hear that, Hinde? In the rich man's house, I saw them serve him an omelet. What do you say to that? That is the food of kings!"

"Did you taste it?"
"God forbid! How should I taste a rich man's omelet?"
"So how do you know?"
"Haven't I eyes? Hinde ... You know just once I'd like you to make me an omelet too."
"What rubbish you are talking . . . Do you know what an omelet is made of? First, the rich use mounds of butter."

"As far as I'm concerned, it can be without butter ... only make me an omelet."
"Even so, but what about eggs? You can't make an omelet without eggs."
"Why talk about eggs in the plural? Just one egg, Hinde."
"And where am I to get one egg? I had one egg in the house and I used the white for the gefilte fish *and glazed* challah *with the yolk."*
"Hinde, Hinde. If you wanted to, you could make me an omelet."
"But how? Maybe I should make it of flour?"
"Make it of flour. The main thing is to make me an omelet."

Mushroom omelet

(shvammen omlett)

1 pound fresh mushrooms or 6-ounce can
2 tablespoons butter or margarine
1 medium onion, chopped
6 eggs
dash of garlic powder
salt and pepper to taste

1 Wash fresh mushrooms thoroughly and pat dry, or drain canned mushrooms. Slice mushrooms.
2 Melt the fat in a large skillet and sauté onions until golden. Add mushrooms and cook until tender.
3 Beat eggs with seasonings and pour over onions and mushrooms. Stir until omelet is set and cook until golden brown.
Serves 3-4

Onion omelet

(fankuchen mit tzibbeles)

2 tablespoons butter or margarine
2 medium onions, minced
6 eggs
salt and pepper to taste

1 In a large skillet, melt the fat and sauté the onions until golden.
2 Beat the eggs with salt and pepper and pour over the onions, stirring until eggs are set.
Serves 3

"And where am I to take flour from? I have no flour either.
"But how? Shall I make it from an onion? Oh, I don't even have onions in the house, but I have a tooth of garlic."
"Then take the garlic, but make me an omelet."
At this point, the poor woman lost patience.

"Suddenly, he wants an omelet. Saw one in the rich man's house, so he also wants one! If the rich man were to cut off his nose — he'd have to cut his nose off too!"
Whereupon she served the garlic and said, "Go and wash your hands. Your omelet is ready."
"What, it's ready so soon?" said her husband. "You really are quick, Hinde. The rich think that the whole world belongs to them but if a poor man has a smart wife, he can eat an omelet too."

Then he tasted the garlic and wrinkled his nose. "Ugh, Hinde, this omelet of yours has an awful taste . . . excuse me, that's not what I meant. The devil knows what the rich find so tasty in an omelet."

●●●

Potato-onion omelet
(fankuchen mit kartoffel un ayer)

1 pound potatoes, peeled
boiling salted water
2 tablespoons butter
1 large onion, coarsely chopped
salt and pepper to taste
6 eggs, beaten

Method I
1 Cube potatoes and cook in boiling salted water to cover until partially tender, about 10 minutes. Drain.
2 Heat fat in large pan and sauté onions until transparent. Reduce heat, add potatoes and salt and pepper and continue cooking 15 minutes, turning the potatoes often.
3 Turn heat up, add eggs and stir omelet until golden brown.

Method II
1 Slice potatoes thinly.
2 Heat fat in a large pan and sauté onions until transparent. Add potatoes and salt and pepper, cover and continue cooking on a low flame 30 minutes, turning potatoes frequently.
3 Add eggs and stir until golden brown.
Serves 4

eggs and salads

●●●

Spicy omelet
(gefefferter fankuchen)

4 fresh tomatoes
2 tablespoons butter
3 medium onions, chopped
1 green pepper, chopped
1 teaspoon cayenne or chili pepper, or to taste
salt to taste
6 eggs, beaten

1 Blanch tomatoes by pouring boiling water over. Let stand 5 minutes, peel and chop. Set aside.
2 Melt the butter in a large skillet and sauté the onions until transparent. Add the tomatoes, peppers and seasonings and stir over a medium flame 15-20 minutes.
3 Stir in the eggs and cook until set, stirring frequently.
Note: This should be prepared as spicy as possible.
Serves 4

Parsley omelet
(petrushka omlett)

6 eggs
½ cup fresh minced parsley
1 tablespoon water
½ teaspoon salt
¼ teaspoon pepper
2 tablespoons butter or margarine

1 Beat the eggs with the parsley, water, salt and pepper.
2 Melt the fat in a large skillet, pour in the mixture, cover and cook on a low flame until set, about 7 minutes.
Serves 3-4

Beet and cucumber salad
(burikes mit iggerkes)

1 pound fresh beets
1 large cucumber, peeled and cubed
1 shallot or small onion, chopped
dash of grated nutmeg
salt to taste
1 ½ cups sour cream

1 Wash beets and remove tops. Place in saucepan, cover with water, bring to a boil and cook until tender, 45 minutes-1 hour. Cool beets and peel. Cut into cubes.
2 Mix beets, cucumber and onions with nutmeg and salt and toss with sour cream.
Serves 6
Color plate facing page 104.

Cucumber and sour cream salad
(iggerkes mit smetene)

2 large cucumbers
½ cup sour cream
1 tablespoon lemon juice
½ teaspoon sugar
¼ teaspoon salt
freshly ground pepper to taste

Slice cucumbers very thin. Mix remaining ingredients, pour over cucumbers and toss.
Serves 3-4

Cabbage salad I
(veisser kroit salat I)

1 medium cabbage head
1 tablespoon prepared mustard
½ teaspoon sugar
½ teaspoon salt
½ cup vinegar
¼ cup oil
¼ cup water

1 Shred cabbage, rinse and drain thoroughly.
2 Mix mustard with sugar, salt and vinegar until smooth. Add oil and water, mix well and pour over cabbage. Toss. Let rest ½ hour before serving.
Serves 4-6
Color plate facing page 104.

Cabbage salad II
(veisser kroit salat II)

1 medium cabbage head
about ½ cup salt
2 tablespoons sugar
1 teaspoon salt
½ cup vinegar
½ cup oil
1 cup water

1 Shred cabbage, rinse and drain. In a crock, alternate layers of cabbage with ½ cup salt. Press down with a heavy weight and let stand overnight.
2 The next day, remove cabbage from crock and drain until almost dry.
3 Mix together remaining ingredients and pour over cabbage. Toss. Let rest ½ hour before serving.
Serves 4-6

Red cabbage salad
(roit-kroit salat)

1 medium red cabbage head
boiling water
1 tablespoon sugar
1 teaspoon salt
½ cup red wine or wine vinegar
½ cup oil
1 cup water

1 Shred cabbage and immerse in boiling water until water boils again. Remove, drain and squeeze dry.
2 Mix the sugar and salt with the wine vinegar. Add oil and water and blend well. Pour over cabbage and toss. Let rest ½ hour before serving.
Note: Leftover dressings can be stored and reused for any of these cabbage salads.
Serves 4-6

Husham, that classic fool of Jewish humor, was once asked, "How many eggs can you eat on an empty stomach?"
Husham pondered on this and finally answered, "Four."
"You fool," mocked the other, "when you've eaten one egg, your stomach isn't empty any more."
Husham laughed heartily and thought this a very clever joke, and the moment he met one of his friends, he asked him, "How many eggs can you eat on an empty stomach?"
"Three!" his friend promptly replied. Husham was very upset. "What a pity!" he said, "If you had guessed four, I'd have had a marvellous answer for you!"

●●●

Celery-tomato-egg salad
(tzelery, tomatten mit ayer un griene tzibbeles)

2 tablespoons mayonnaise
1 tablespoon sour cream
1 teaspoon prepared mustard
salt and pepper to taste
3 stalks celery, thinly sliced
1 large tomato, diced
2 hard-boiled eggs, diced
1 small onion, diced

Blend the mayonnaise, sour cream, mustard and salt and pepper. Toss with the remaining ingredients.
Serves 4

These popular Eastern European salads are served as sidedishes. Pictured from top to bottom: Cabbage salad I (page 102) and Beet and cucumber salad (page 101).

▶

A wealthy man was once asked,
"How did you get so rich?"
"I kept two rules," he answered. "Whatever I had to do the next day — I did that very day. Whatever I was going to eat that day — I ate the next day."

Two Jews were finishing their dinner in a restaurant. The waiter came over to them and asked, "Will you be wanting anything else? A glass of tea, maybe?"
"Good", answered one, "bring me a glass of tea."
"You can bring me a glass of tea too," answered the second, "but see to it that the glass is clean."
The waiter went to the kitchen and soon returned holding a tray with two glasses.
"Excuse me, gentlemen," he said to the two diners, "which one of you wanted a clean glass?"

Red cole slaw with green pepper
(kroit salat mit griene feffer)

1 medium red cabbage
½ teaspoon salt
2 green peppers, cut in thin strips
2 large onions, sliced in thin rings
pepper to taste
½ cup cider vinegar or lemon juice
½ cup cold water

1 Quarter and wash cabbage. Shred finely, sprinkle with the salt and let stand 1 hour.
2 Crush cabbage lightly with hands. Place in bowl with peppers and onions, season with pepper and adjust salt. Mix vinegar or lemon juice with the water, sprinkle over vegetables and toss.
3 Pack into 1 ½-2-quart jar, cover and refrigerate 2 days before serving. Will keep in refrigerator 1 week-10 days.
Serves 6

An integral part of the Shabbat meal is Golden chicken soup (page 34) garnished with Kreplach (page 116) and served with Challah (page 130).

Eggplant salad I
(sinias salat I)

½ cup oil
1 large onion, chopped
1 large eggplant, peeled and cubed
½ cup fresh chopped parsley
3 ounces tomato paste diluted in ½ cup water
juice of 1 lemon
chili powder to taste
salt to taste

1 Heat 1 tablespoon of the oil in a large skillet and sauté onions until transparent. Remove onions with a slotted spoon and set aside.
2 Add the rest of the oil to the skillet and sauté eggplant cubes until tender, about 10-15 minutes.
3 Put eggplant through a meat grinder, or mash. Mix with onions and remaining ingredients. Season to taste, chill and serve cold.

Eggplant salad II

(sinias salat II)

1 medium onion, diced
¼ cup oil
1 medium eggplant, cubed
3 ounces tomato paste diluted in ½ cup water
2 garlic cloves, crushed
salt and pepper to taste
½ cup fresh chopped parsley or dill

1 Sauté onions in oil until transparent. Remove onions and
  add eggplant cubes. Sauté until soft and remove from heat.
2 In a small saucepan, mix diluted tomato paste with onions,
  and salt and pepper. Simmer 10 minutes. Remove from heat,
  pour over eggplant and garnish with parsley or dill. Serve
  either hot or cold.
Serves 4

Tomatoes stuffed with eggs and scallions
(gefilte tomatten)

6 hard-boiled eggs, chopped
½ cup finely chopped scallions
3 tablespoons mayonnaise
salt and pepper to taste
6 firm tomatoes
6 black olives

1 Mix the eggs, scallions, mayonnaise and salt and pepper.
2 Cut tomatoes in 8 equal sections within 1 inch of the bottom. Spread out on a plate like a flower. Top with egg mixture and garnish with olives. Chill before serving.
Serves 6

Tongue salad
(tzung salat)

2 cups leftover tongue, chopped
2 cups boiled potatoes, peeled and diced
2 cups apples, peeled, cored and diced
2 dill pickles, diced
2/3 cup mayonnaise
1 tablespoon hot mustard
2 tablespoons white vinegar
½ teaspoon chopped fresh dill
or ¼ teaspoon dried dill weed
salt and pepper to taste

1 In a mixing bowl, combine tongue, potatoes, apples and pickles.
2 In a separate bowl, blend together the mayonnaise, mustard, vinegar, dill and salt and pepper. Pour over tongue mixture. Toss well before serving.
Serves 8

dumplings

and filled doughs

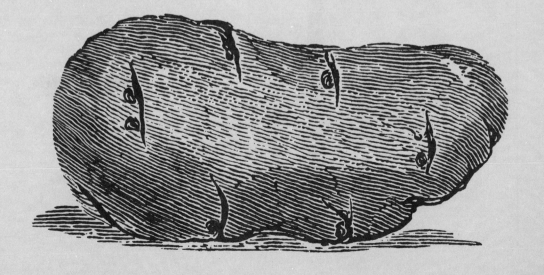

dumplings
and filled doughs

The Tzaddik, Rabbi Abraham Heshel was opposed to having too many fast days. Once, when he was on his travels with his disciples they happened to arrive at a small town where a fast day had been proclaimed by the Jewish community because of the drought. The Rabbi did not observe this fast and sat down with his Hassidim to eat and drink. This news soon spread throughout the town and caused a great uproar.
"How could you break a public fast, when the drought is so severe and we need rain so badly?" asked the local Jews bitterly.
"How foolish you are," retorted the Rabbi. "You need rain so that you can grow enough to eat and drink, don't you? So now you are fasting and showing the Holy One, blessed be He, that you can do without food and drink. On the contrary, you should eat and drink and show the Lord above that you cannot exist without — so he will have mercy on you and will send the rain."

Dumplings
(galushkes)

2 eggs
2 teaspoons salt
½ cup water
2½ cups flour
2 quarts salted water

1 Beat eggs with salt and ½ cup cold water. Add gradually to flour, beating well after each addition to form a sticky dough. Dust hands with flour and roll out half the dough in a ½-inch-thick rope. Repeat procedure with other half.
2 Bring salted water to a boil, dip a sharp knife into the boiling water and slice dough into small pieces. Drop into boiling water and cook 10 minutes from the time they rise to the surface. Remove with slotted spoon. Serve dumplings hot with Goulash (page 49), smothered in sauce, or with any meat that has a sauce. To reheat, lightly sauté dumplings in a small amount of oil in a covered skillet.
Note: This is an Eastern European Jewish adaptation of the Middle European dumplings known as *nockerl*. They were often enhanced by frying in bread crumbs.
Makes about 40 dumplings

Color plate facing page 33.

Potato dumplings
(kartoffel knaydel)

3 pounds potatoes, peeled
2 large eggs, beaten
1¼ cups flour
½ cup fresh chopped parsley
salt and pepper to taste
boiling salted water

1 Cook one third of the potatoes in boiling salted water to cover until very soft, about 20-25 minutes. Drain.
2 Meanwhile, coarsely grate remaining potatoes and drain thoroughly.
3 Mash cooked potatoes with grated potatoes and mix in eggs, flour, parsley and salt and pepper. With wet hands, form into 1-inch balls. Drop into a large kettle or saucepan filled with boiling salted water. As soon as dumplings rise to the surface, cover and continue boiling 10 minutes longer. Remove with slotted spoon.
Makes about 30 dumplings

Matzo meal dumplings
(matza-mayl knaydlech)

3 large eggs
1 teaspoon salt
dash of ginger
3 tablespoons oil
6 heaping tablespoons matzo meal
boiling salted water

1 Beat eggs with salt, ginger and oil. Gradually add matzo meal and mix until dough is firm. Let dough rest 1 hour.
2 Wet hands and form dough into 1½-inch balls. Gently place in boiling salted water and simmer 20 minutes. Serve with Golden chicken soup (page 34).
Makes about 12 dumplings

Rabbi Mordecai would never eat a thing in the morning until he had fed a poor man or done some other good deed for the needy. When he was asked to explain this custom, he said, "The Talmud tells us that 'a man has two hearts before he has eaten or drunk.' That means that when a person is hungry he can understand another hungry man. But when he has eaten and drunk his fill, he can no longer understand another's hunger pangs."

●●●

dumplings
and filled doughs

A group of wealthy grain merchants came to consult the Tzaddik, Rabbi Dovidel, for there had been a drought the previous year and the price of wheat had sky rocketed. Expecting the price to rise still higher, they had stored a large quantity of wheat in their granaries. However, the crops that year were plentiful and the price had fallen badly. What were they to do? The Rabbi heard them, meditated on their question and replied, "The Lord above, blessed be His name, who fed and sustained the poor in a year of famine, will feed and sustain the rich in a year of plenty."

●●●

Knishes
(knishes)

Potato dough

3 medium potatoes, boiled, peeled and riced
3 eggs, beaten
2½-3 cups sifted, all-purpose flour
1 teaspoon salt
filling (see page 114)
1 egg yolk

1 Mix riced potatoes with eggs until smooth. Sift in flour and salt and beat well until thoroughly blended.
2 Turn dough onto lightly floured board. Roll out to 1/8-inch thickness and cut into strips 3 inches wide by 6 inches long.
3 Preheat oven to moderate (350°F.).
4 Place 2 tablespoons of the filling (see illustrations on page 113) in the center of each knish and pinch edges closed. Brush tops with egg yolk mixed with 1 tablespoon water and place on well-greased cookie sheet. Bake until golden brown, about 25 minutes.
Makes about 30 knishes

Pastry dough

2 cups all-purpose flour
1 teaspoon baking powder
½ teaspoon salt
2 tablespoons water
1 tablespoon melted chicken fat or oil
2 eggs, well beaten
filling (see page 114)
1 egg yolk

1 Sift together flour, baking powder and salt. Make a well in the center and add water, fat or oil and eggs. Beat until smooth.
2 Turn dough onto lightly floured board and roll out to 1/8 inch thickness. Cut into rounds or squares.
3 Preheat oven to moderate (350°F.).
4 Fill each knish with 2 tablespoons of the filling (see page 114). Moisten edges, fold over and press closed. Brush with egg yolk diluted with 1 tablespoon water. Place in well-greased baking pan and bake about 25 minutes or until golden brown.
Makes about 18 knishes

How to make knishes with potato dough

1 *Roll dough out thinly into an oblong shape and cut into 3 x 6-inch sections.*

2 - 3 *Drop 1 tablespoon of potato filling in the center of each section, or spread with meat filling.*

4 *Press edges closed.*

dumplings
and filled doughs

Fillings for knishes

Potato filling

2 tablespoons chicken fat or oil
2 large onions, chopped coarsely
2 cups mashed potatoes
½ cup *grieben* (optional) (page 64).
salt and pepper to taste

Heat fat or oil in a small skillet and sauté onions until golden brown. Put in mixing bowl, add potatoes and mix in grieben. Add additional oil or fat if necessary to make a sticky texture. Season with salt and pepper.

Kasha filling

1 egg, lightly beaten
1 cup buckwheat (kasha)
2/3 cup boiling water
2 tablespoons chicken fat or oil
2 onions, chopped coarsely
salt and pepper to taste

1 Preheat oven to hot (450°F.).
2 Mix egg with kasha, place in greased baking pan and toast in oven until completely dry, about 10 minutes.
3 Transfer to a double boiler, pour in boiling water and simmer over a medium flame 10-15 minutes.
4 Heat fat or oil in a skillet and sauté onions until golden brown. Add to kasha, season with salt and pepper to taste and mix well.

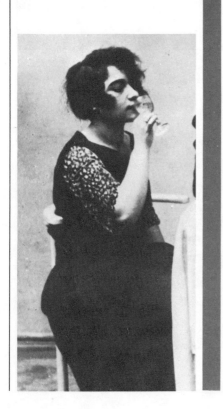

Cheese kreplach
(kayz kreplach)

Dough

3 cups flour
3 teaspoons baking powder
1 teaspoon salt
1 cup sour cream, room temperature
2 eggs, beaten
4 tablespoons melted butter
filling (see below)

1 Sift together flour, baking powder and salt. Mix sour cream, eggs and melted butter. Combine dry ingredients with sour cream mixture.
2 Preheat oven to moderate (350°F.).
3 On a floured surface, roll out dough to 1/8-inch thickness and cut out 4-inch squares. Put 1 tablespoon of the filling (see below) in the center of each square and fold on the diagonal to form a triangle. Pinch edges firmly. (See illustrations on page 117).
4 Place kreplach on greased cookie sheet or shallow baking pan and bake 30-35 minutes or until crust is golden brown. Serve either hot or cold. May be topped with sour cream.
Makes about 18 kreplach

Filling

¼ pound cottage cheese
¼ pound cream cheese, softened
1 egg beaten
1 tablespoon melted butter

Combine all ingredients and mix well.

dumplings
and filled doughs

When the housewife doesn't know what to do with yesterday's leftover meat, she makes kreplach.

●●●

Kreplach
(kreplach)

Dough

2 eggs, beaten
¼ cup water
1 ½ cups flour
¼ teaspoon salt
fillings (see below)
boiling salted water

1 Combine eggs, water, flour and salt and knead into a soft, sticky dough.
2 Roll out dough as thin as possible on a floured surface and cut into 2-inch squares. Add flour as needed.
3 Place 1 teaspoon of the filling (see below) on each square and fold dough over diagonally to form a triangle. Pinch edges firmly together.
4 Place kreplach in a large kettle filled with boiling salted water, cover and cook 20-25 minutes. Serve in a clear soup such as Golden chicken soup (page 34) or Meat soup (page 33).

Fillings for kreplach

Chicken or meat

1 tablespoon oil
1 small onion, chopped
1 cup cooked chicken or meat, ground
1 egg, beaten
salt and pepper to taste

Heat oil, sauté onions until golden and combine with rest of ingredients.

Liver
1 tablespoon oil
1 small onion, chopped
1 cup cooked chicken or beef liver, ground
1 egg, beaten
salt and pepper to taste

Heat oil, sauté onions until golden and combine with rest of ingredients.
Makes about 30 kreplach
Color plate facing page 105

How to make kreplach with meat filling

1 - 2 *Place filling in the center of each square and fold over on the diagonal to form a triangle. Press edges closed.*

3 - 4 *Grasp ends with fingers and pinch together.*

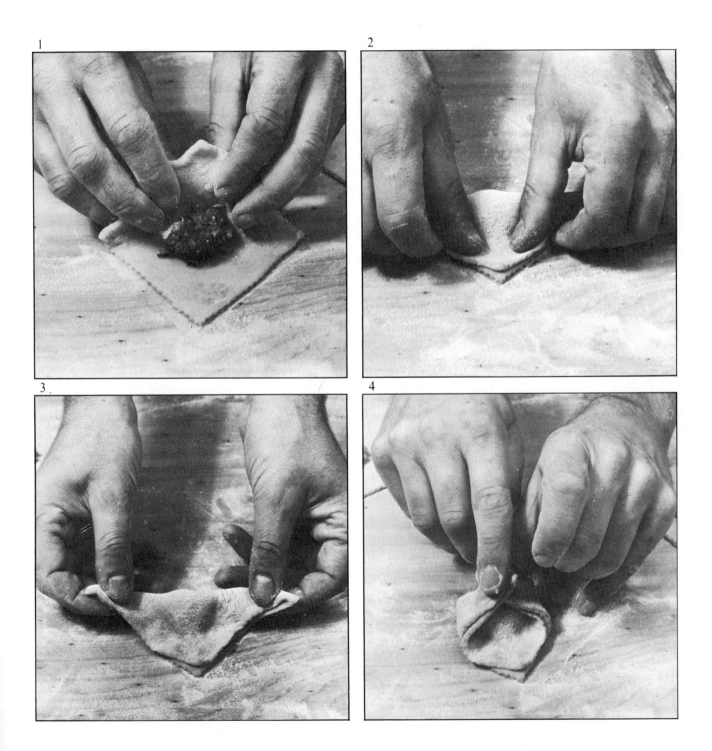

Even if you eat pirogen *all the time, you'll get tired of them in the end.*

●●●●●●●●●●●

When the flour is finished, the quarrel begins.

●●●●●●●●●●●

On the eve of Yom Kippur, Jews eat the meal before the fast, and then at sunset, clear off the table, spread a clean cloth on it and lay volumes of the holy writings on the table until the end of the fast. This is symbolic of the fact that Yom Kippur is spent, not in eating and drinking, but in the study of Torah and in prayer.

●●●●●●●●●●●

There's nothing better than a good feast.

●●●

Pirogen
(pirogen)

Dough

1 cup all-purpose flour
¾ teaspoon salt
¼ teaspoon pepper
½ cup mashed potatoes
½ cup shortening
1 egg, well beaten
filling (see page 120)
salted water
oil

1 Sift flour with salt and pepper. Mix in potatoes.
2 Cut in shortening until dough is flaky. Make a well in the center and work in egg.
3 Turn dough onto lightly floured board and knead until smooth and elastic. If necessary, add more flour to make a stiff dough. Form into a ball and roll out to a thickness of ¼ inch. Cut into 3-inch rounds.
4 Fill each round with 1 tablespoon of the filling and stretch dough to cover. Pinch edges together to seal, forming a half-moon.
5 Fill a large kettle with salted water and bring to a boil. Carefully add pirogen and boil 5 minutes. Remove with a slotted spoon and drain.
6 Pour a layer of oil in a large skillet and heat over a high flame. When hot, fry pirogen on both sides until golden brown.
Makes about 18 pirogen

How to make pirogen

1 *Cut dough into rounds with a glass and spoon filling in center.*
2 *Fold dough over and press edges closed.*
3 *Place carefully in a kettle of boiling water; boil 5 minutes and drain.*
4 *Fry quicky in hot oil on both sides.*

dumplings
and filled doughs

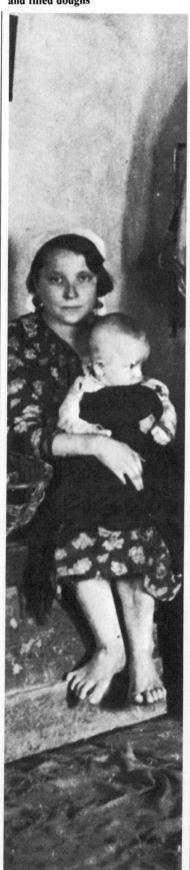

Fillings for Pirogen

Meat-onion

1 tablespoon oil
2 onions, minced
2 garlic cloves, minced
1 pound ground beef or veal
1 teaspoon sage
salt and pepper to taste
1 egg, beaten

1 In a large skillet, heat the oil and sauté the onions until golden brown. Add garlic and ground meat. Season with the sage and salt and pepper and cook until the meat is well browned.
2 Add egg to meat mixture, blend in well and cook until set.

Potato-onion

4 tablespoons chicken fat
½ cup minced onions
2 cups mashed potatoes
salt and pepper to taste
1 egg, slightly beaten

1 Melt 1 tablespoon of the fat and sauté onions until golden brown.
2 Add onions to potatoes, season with salt and pepper and work in remaining fat. Add egg and mix well.

What can a man lose as long as he lives? He might as well eat blintzes *in the meantime.*

Your own kasha *is tastier than a sizzling roast on a stranger's table.*

Even dogs eat pie at Purim.

Don't put the cat in charge of the cream.

Love is sweet as long as there is bread to go with it.

Too many cooks burn the pot.

Sweet cheese

1 pound farmer cheese
2 eggs, separated
2 tablespoons sugar
2 tablespoons honey
1 tablespoon bread crumbs
½ teaspoon salt

1 Blend cheese with egg yolks. Add sugar, honey, bread crumbs and salt and mix well.
2 Beat egg whites until stiff. Fold into cheese mixture.

pancakes and breads

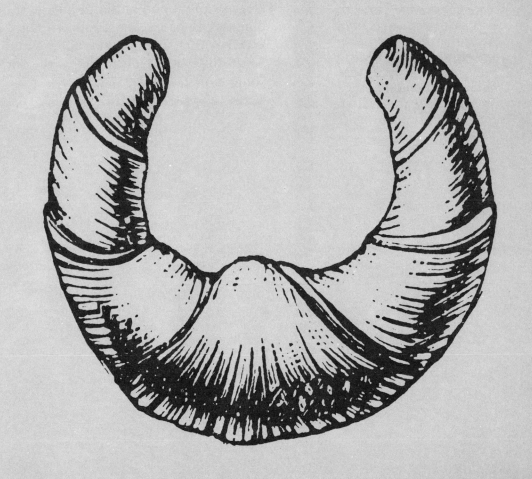

The custom of eating dairy foods at Shavuoth has never been sufficiently explained, though various commentators have offered many possible reasons. There are some who say that when Moses was born and his mother hid him in the bulrushes of the Nile in Egypt, the daughter of Pharaoh found and took him out of the water on the exact date of Shavuoth. And though he was a tiny baby he refused the milk of an Egyptian wet nurse so that they brought his mother to nurse him. Dairy foods at Shavuoth, some say, are eaten in memory of that event.
Others say that the Children of Israel received the Torah at Mount Sinai on Shavuoth, when they were commanded to eat only kosher meat. At that point they had no kosher vessels or kosher meat so they had to make do with dairy foods and, in memory of that event, we too, eat dairy foods on the Shavuoth festival.

Blintzes
(blintzes)

Batter

1 cup sifted all-purpose flour
½ teaspoon salt
pinch of sugar
1 egg, beaten
1 ½ cups cold water
butter
filling (see page 125)

1 Combine flour, salt, sugar, egg and water and blend thoroughly with a mixer until smooth.
2 Heat a medium-sized skillet over a high flame and brush with a small amount of butter. Pour enough of the batter to barely coat pan bottom and tilt immediately so that batter spreads over entire bottom of pan. Cook until batter stops bubbling and edges begin to lift. Slide pancakes out onto a towel, cooked side up. Repeat process until all the batter is used.
3 Place 1 tablespoon of the filling (see page 125) in the center of each pancake and roll up or fold sides over to form an envelope.
4 Heat 1 tablespoon butter in a large skillet and fry several blintzes at once, seam side down, until golden brown. Turn and fry other side. Repeat, adding more butter as necessary. Serve blintzes hot, garnished with sour cream or confectioners' sugar.
Makes about 12 blintzes

Fillings for Blintzes

Apple

2 cooking apples, peeled, cored and finely grated
1 tablespoon bread crumbs
½ cup ground almonds
1 egg, beaten
1 tablespoon confectioners' sugar
½ teaspoon cinnamon
¼ teaspoon nutmeg
¼ teaspoon ground cloves

Mix all ingredients together thoroughly.

Cheese

1 cup cottage cheese or softened cream cheese
1 egg, beaten
1 teaspoon sugar
dash of salt

Mix all ingredients together thoroughly.

Russian buckwheat pancakes
(russishe kashe latkes)

2 cups buckwheat flour
½ cup sifted all-purpose flour
1 teaspoon baking powder
1 teaspoon salt
¼ teaspoon sugar
3 cups warm milk
2 eggs
butter

1 Sift the dry ingredients together. Mix with milk and eggs until batter is smooth. Let batter rest ½ hour.
2 Heat a medium-sized skillet and brush with butter. Pour in 1 tablespoon of the batter and tilt the pan immediately so that batter spreads over entire bottom of the pan. Cook pancakes on both sides until golden brown. Grease the pan for each pancake. Serve with sour cream, jelly or honey.
Makes about 20 pancakes

The tradition of eating pancakes and donuts fried in oil on Chanukah, originates with the story told in the Talmud of the miracle which took place with a flask of oil. When the Greeks overran the Temple, they defiled all the oil and when the Hasmoneans conquered them, they were able to find only one flask of pure oil which was sufficient to burn in the Temple lamp for only one day. Miraculously, the oil burned for eight days! That is why we kindle Chanukah lights for eight days amid rejoicing and feasting.

●●●●●●●●●●●●

A beloved maiden is milk. A bride is butter. A wife is cheese. (Ludwig Borne)

●●●

125

pancakes and breads

In Chelm, the town of fools, the Town Council once sat for seven days and nights and finally resolved to send a delegation out into the wide world to see if there was something worth bringing back to Chelm. The delegation from Chelm wandered around the world for a long time and saw nothing they considered worthwhile introducing into Chelm, except for one thing they saw in Vilna. Now, what was Vilna famous for? For its fine bagels, of course. The Chelmans had never seen nor tasted anything like these delicious rings of crusty dough. After each delegate had eaten at least two dozen bagels, the senior member exclaimed, "I am an old man, but never in all my life have I tasted any food as delicious as this."

Then and there the delegation decided to learn how to make bagels and to bring the secret back to their home town. They went to the baker and promised to pay him any price if he agreed to teach them how to make bagels. The baker told them that there was nothing easier. "Take some round holes, put some dough around them, simmer them in a pot of boiling water, then pop them in the oven and out will come your bagels."

The Chelmans were still puzzled. "But where do we get the holes?" they asked.

Sour cream pancakes I
(smetene latkes I)

1 cup milk
1 cup sour cream
1 cup all-purpose flour
2/3 teaspoon baking soda
pinch of salt
shortening as needed

1 Mix together the milk, sour cream, flour, baking soda and salt.
2 Melt the shortening in a large skillet and, when hot, drop in the batter by the tablespoonful. When bubbles appear and pancake is golden brown, turn and fry the other side. Add more shortening if necessary. Pancakes will have a soft consistency. Keep warm in slow oven (200°F.) until ready to serve.
Serve with jam or syrup, or sprinkled with confectioners' sugar.
Serves 4

Sour cream pancakes II
(smetene latkes II)

1 cup sifted all-purpose flour
½ teaspoon baking soda
½ teaspoon salt
2 tablespoons sugar
1½ cups sour cream
2 eggs, beaten
½ cup water
butter or margarine

1 Combine dry ingredients. Add sour cream and eggs and mix until batter is smooth. Stir in ½ cup cold water and let batter rest for ½ hour.
2 Heat a medium-size skillet and brush with butter or margarine. Pour in a serving spoon of the batter and tilt pan immediately so that batter spreads over entire bottom of pan. Cook pancakes on both sides until golden brown. Grease pan for each pancake. Serve with maple syrup, jelly, honey or sugar.
Makes 8 pancakes

126

"First you buy the bagels from me," explained the baker, "then you eat them and use the holes again to make more bagels."

So, all the delegates bought themselves strings of bagels which they hung round their necks. They paid the bagel baker for his lesson and happily set out for Chelm. On the way they came to a steep mountain slope, where the dean of the group exhorted them, "Fellow Chelmans, we must observe our tradition of not carrying anything down a slope which can roll down by itself."

So, the members of the delegation took off their bagel necklaces and threw them off the top of the slope so that they could roll down by themselves.

Now at the foot of that hill there happened to be a pack of hungry dogs who smelled the bagels and began devouring them.

When the Chelmans came down the slope and saw what the dogs were doing, they began to shout, "Never mind the bagels, but please be careful with the holes! For heavens' sake, please don't touch the holes!"

But dogs will be dogs and as they wolfed down the bagels, they paid no attention to the holes. Alas, the Chelmans searched high and low, but couldn't find a single hole.

Potato pancakes
(kartoffel latkes)

6 medium potatoes
1 small onion
2 eggs, lightly beaten
3 tablespoons flour
1 teaspoon salt
¼ teaspoon pepper
½ teaspoon baking powder
cooking oil

1 Peel and grate potatoes, squeeze out liquid and place in mixing bowl. Grate onion, squeeze out liquid and add to potatoes. Blend well. Stir in eggs and add flour, salt, pepper and baking powder. Mix well.
2 Heat oil to cover bottom of a large skillet. When hot (but not smoking), drop in potato batter by the heaping tablespoonful. Brown on both sides, turning once. Drain on absorbent paper towels. Add oil as needed. Keep warm in a slow (200°F.) oven.
Latkes are traditionally served with applesauce or sour cream.
Serves 6
Color plate facing page 128.

pancakes and breads

Mournful and downcast, the delegation trudged back to Chelm, with no bagels and no holes and because of this, there are no bagels in Chelm to this very day.

●●●●●●●●●●●

When you eat a bagel, where does the hole go? Into your pocket!

●●●●●●●●●●●

Bread from the hands of strangers chokes you.

●●●●●●●●●●●

If you're unlucky, your bread always falls down on the buttered side.

●●●

Bagels
(baygel)

1 envelope dry yeast or 1 compressed cake
¼ cup lukewarm water
1 cup scalded milk
¼ cup butter
1 tablespoon sugar
1 teaspoon salt
4 cups sifted, all-purpose flour
1 egg, separated
2 tablespoons cold water
coarse salt (optional)
poppy seeds (optional)

1 Dissolve yeast in lukewarm water. Set aside for 5 minutes.
2 Pour scalded milk into deep mixing bowl and blend in butter, sugar and salt. Stir in yeast and sift in flour a little at a time.
3 Beat egg white until stiff and gently fold into dough. Reserve yolk. Mix dough well and turn onto lightly floured board. Let rest for 10 minutes, then knead for 5 minutes. Shape into a ball and place in greased mixing bowl. Cover with a damp cloth and let rise in a warm place until doubled in bulk, about 1 hour.
4 Preheat oven to hot (400°F.).
5 Punch down and turn onto lightly floured board. Separate dough into small balls and roll each ball into 5-inch ropes about the width of a finger. Let rest on board for 10 minutes.
6 Bring a kettle filled with water to a rolling boil, reduce heat to simmer and carefully drop bagels in one at a time. Cook on both sides 1 minute. Remove and drain.
7 Place bagels on a well-greased cookie sheet. Beat reserved egg yolk with cold water and brush over bagels. If desired, sprinkle with coarse salt and/or poppy seeds. Bake until brown, about 45 minutes.
Makes about 3 dozen small bagels

Potatoes play an important role in the Yiddish kitchen. Pictured from top to bottom: Fried potato balls (page 168), Potato bake (page 90) and Potato pancakes (page 127). ▶

How to make bagels

1 *Roll each ball of dough into 5-inch ropes.*
2 *Pinch edges together to form rings. Let rest 10 minutes.*
3 *Carefully place into simmering water.*
4 *Remove with a spatula to a well-greased cooky sheet.*

During Pesach, try Matzo meal chicken (page 162), with Matzo dumplings (page 164) and Carrot/prune casserole (page 163).

There was once a woman who bought bagels every day. As time went on, she noticed that they were getting smaller and smaller, so she went to the baker and complained. "I could understand if you were to make the loaves smaller — then you'd earn more — but why should you mind if the holes are the same size?"

●●●●●●●●●●●●

A Tzaddik was once told that a man in his town had died of hunger. He could not understand this and asked, "How is it possible? If he had turned to me or to anyone else, we would surely have shared our bread with him."
"But Rabbi," came the reply, "that man was once wealthy, so he was ashamed to ask for anything from his fellow-man."
"In that case," said the Tzaddik, "he died not from hunger but from arrogance."

●●●

Challah
(challah)

6 tablespoons shortening
1½ cups boiling water
2 tablespoons sugar
3 teaspoons salt
2 envelopes dry yeast or 2 compressed cakes
½ cup lukewarm water
3 eggs, well beaten, plus 1 egg yolk
7 cups sifted, all-purpose flour
poppy seeds (optional)

1 Melt shortening in boiling water and pour into mixing bowl. Add sugar and salt and set aside to cool.
2 Dissolve yeast in lukewarm water. Let stand for about 1 minute. Stir in the 3 well-beaten eggs. Add to water-shortening mixture.
3 Sift in 4 cups of flour a little at a time. Mix well. Add 3 additional cups of flour and work in well. Let dough rest for 10 minutes.
4 Place on floured board and knead for at least 10 minutes until dough is smooth and elastic.
5 Shape dough into a ball and place in clean mixing bowl. Grease the surface, cover with a damp cloth and let rise in warm place for 2 hours or until doubled in bulk.
6 Punch dough down, remove to lightly floured board and knead again for a few minutes until texture is fine.
7 Divide dough into 9 equal parts. Roll each part into a long strand. Join 3 strands together and braid. Do the same with the other strands. Place each of the 3 braided loaves in a greased loaf pan.
8 Preheat oven to moderate (375°F.).
9 Brush tops with egg yolk mixed with 1 tablespoon water. Sprinkle with poppy seeds, if desired. Set aside to rise in a warm place for 45 minutes.
10 Bake about 50 minutes or until loaves are lightly browned and sound hollow when tapped.
Makes 3 loaves
Color plate facing page 49

How to braid a challah

1 *For each loaf, separate dough into 3 equal sections. Roll each section into a long strand.*

2 - 3 *Pinch strands together at one end and braid.*

4 *Pinch ends firmly together.*

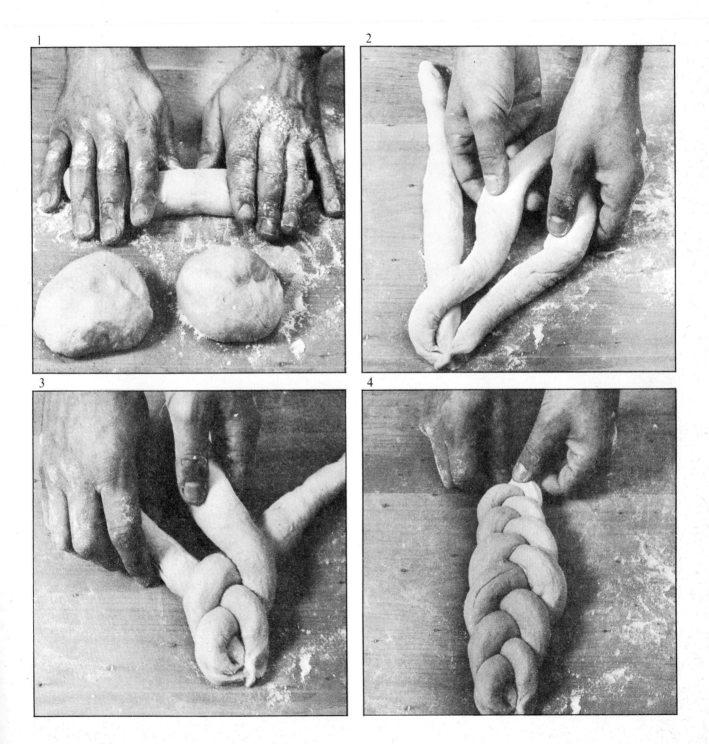

pancakes and breads

P

The festive meal served for Rosh Hashanah among Eastern European Jews was chock-full of symbolism. Some women used to bake special challoth in the form of ladders, based on ancient teachings which taught that the Holy One, blessed be He, hangs ladders in the firmament for souls to ascend or descend as God decrees.

Other women would make their challoth in the form of birds, symbolizing the words of the Prophet Isaiah, Chapter 31, verse 5, "As birds flying, so will the Lord of Hosts defend Jerusalem."

In Lithuania, they made challoth in the shape of crowns, in accordance with the Rosh Hashanah prayer, "the whole world will crown Thee." It is also customary to eat challah dipped in honey and apples dipped in honey at the Rosh Hashanah meal, to ensure a sweet new year.

There are some communities who observe the custom of eating the head of a fish, a chicken or a sheep at Rosh Hashanah, as a symbol of their prayers to God to put them at the head, not at the tail. Many Jews take care not to eat sour or bitter foods at Rosh Hashanah, so that the coming year will be sweet and happy.

●●●

Sweet challah for the high holidays
(yontovdige ziesse challah)

2 envelopes dry yeast or 2 compressed cakes
1 cup lukewarm water
3½ tablespoons sugar
4 cups sifted, all-purpose flour
2 teaspoons salt
2 eggs, well beaten, plus 1 egg yolk
3 tablespoons oil
½ cup raisins

1 Mix yeast with ¼ cup of the lukewarm water. Set aside for 5 minutes. Add a pinch of sugar and let stand 10 minutes longer.
2 In a large mixing bowl, sift the flour with the salt. With your fist, make a well in the flour and pour in the yeast. Add the remaining sugar, 2 eggs and remaining water. Beat well.
3 Add the oil and work in. If the dough is too sticky, sprinkle lightly with a little flour.
4 Turn dough onto a lightly floured board. Slap the dough against the board for 2-3 minutes. Knead the dough for 5 minutes, or until smooth and elastic. Gently fold in the raisins. Shape dough into a ball.
5 Grease the dough and place in a clean mixing bowl. Cover with a damp cloth and let rise in a warm place for 2 hours, or until doubled in bulk.
5 Punch down dough, remove from bowl and return to lightly floured board. Knead for about 3 minutes. Return to bowl, cover with damp cloth and let rise for about 45 minutes.
7 Punch down dough again. Place on board and cut in two. Roll each section into a strand about 2 feet long. Curl each strand into a snail shape. Place on greased cookie sheet.
8 Preheat oven to moderate (350°F.).
9 Cover with a damp cloth and let rise in a warm place for ½ hour. Just before baking, brush the tops with 1 egg yolk mixed with 1 tablespoon water. Bake 50 minutes or until golden brown.
Makes 2 loaves

cakes, pastries, cookies

Chocolate yeast cake
(babke)

1 envelope dry yeast or 1 compressed cake
1 cup lukewarm milk
4-5 cups sifted, all-purpose flour
¾ cup sugar
¼ teaspoon salt
½ cup butter
3 eggs, beaten, room temperature
8 ounces (squares) bittersweet chocolate
3 tablespoons strong black coffee
½ cup raisins
melted butter

1 Dissolve yeast in 3 tablespoons of the milk. Let rest for 5 minutes.
2 In a large mixing bowl, sift together 1 cup of the flour with 1 teaspoon sugar and the salt. Stir in remaining milk. Add yeast, mix well and cover with a damp cloth. Put in a warm place to rise until dough becomes very light in texture, about 45 minutes.
3 Cream butter with remaining sugar. Add to dough and blend in the eggs. Sift in remaining flour and mix until very smooth and pliable, adding more flour as necessary.
4 Melt chocolate over a double boiler. Stir in coffee and raisins.
5 Spread dough on a lightly floured pastry board. Coat with chocolate mixture. Roll dough as for a jelly roll and slice in half.
6 Preheat oven to moderate (375°F.).
7 Place each roll in a well-greased loaf pan, cover with a damp cloth and let rise in a warm place until doubled in bulk, about 45 minutes.
8 Brush tops with melted butter and bake 35 minutes.
Makes 2 cakes

A Jewish family once invited a poor man to their Chanukah meal. The traditional latkes were served and the guest quickly took one and said, "This one is in honor of the Lord of the Universe." Then he took two, saying, "I'll eat these two in honor of Moses and Aaron." Next, he took three in honor of the three patriarchs, Abraham, Isaac and Jacob, then four to honor the four matriarchs, Sarah, Rebecca, Rachel and Leah — and so he went on till the host turned to his wife and said, "You'd better take the platter of latkes away, he may want to honor the six hundred thousand that Moses led out of Egypt..."

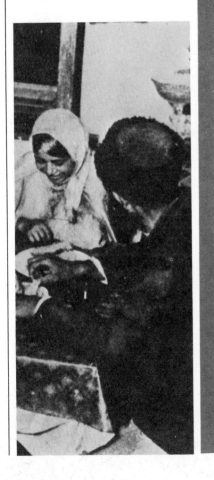

Honey cake I
(honig lekach I)

4 eggs, beaten
1 ½ cups honey, preferably dark
1 cup brown sugar
1 cup strong coffee
2 teaspoons oil
grated rind and juice of 1 orange
3 ½ cups sifted, all-purpose flour
4 teaspoons baking powder
1 teaspoon ground allspice
1 teaspoon cinnamon
dash of salt

1 Preheat oven to moderate (325°F.).
2 Mix together eggs, honey, sugar, coffee, oil and orange rind and juice.
3 Mix flour with baking powder, allspice, cinnamon and salt. Gradually add to egg mixture and blend thoroughly.
4 Pour into 2 greased loaf pans and bake 1 hour. *Lekach* is traditionally served with hot tea.
Makes 2 loaves

Honey cake II
(honig lekach II)

5 eggs
1 cup brown sugar
1 cup honey
2 tablespoons cooking oil
½ cup raisins
1 teaspoon ground ginger
½ teaspoon allspice
½ teaspoon cinnamon
3 cups all-purpose flour
1 teaspoon baking powder
1 teaspoon baking soda
1 cup cold strong coffee

1 Preheat oven to slow (300°F.).
2 Beat eggs with sugar. Add honey, oil, raisins, ginger, allspice and cinnamon. Mix well.
3 Sift flour with baking powder and soda and add to egg-sugar mixture, alternating with coffee. Stir until batter is smooth and well blended.
4 Line a large baking pan with greased brown paper or wax paper. Bake 1 hour or until done. Cool. Turn cake upside down on a wire rack and peel off paper.
Makes 1 cake

A Jewish lady once received some visitors and proudly served the lekach she had made. Her friends sat and chatted, eating the cake all the time. Finally, one of the guests got up to go and said to her hostess, "Your lekach is really excellent. Imagine, I ate three slices!"
"You ate five," answered her hostess, "but who's counting?"

Vodka doesn't go sour and shtrudel doesn't get stale.

Man is like a fly — he rushes to the honey.

Honey cake III
(honig lekach III)

excellent
made with no nut
yellow raisins
10/98

4 eggs
1 cup sugar
3 tablespoons melted margarine
1 cup honey
1 cup strong coffee
3 cups sifted, all-purpose flour
1 ½ teaspoons baking powder
1 teaspoon baking soda
1 cup chopped walnuts or almonds
1 teaspoon cinnamon
½ teaspoon ground ginger
½ teaspoon ground allspice

1 Preheat oven to moderate (350°F.).
2 Beat the eggs with the sugar and margarine.
3 Combine the honey and coffee and blend into the egg-sugar mixture.
4 Sift flour with baking powder and soda. Blend into the egg mixture. Add the nuts and the spices and mix well.
5 Line a 9 x 12-inch cake pan with greased brown paper or wax paper. Bake 1 hour. Cool. Turn cake upside down on a wire rack and peel off paper.
Makes 1 cake

In Chelm, the Polish town of proverbially stupid people, there was once a very poor teacher, a melamed, who taught children in his own home.

During the year, he would visit the splendid mansions of the rich to collect his meager salary. It so happened that one year his visit fell during the Shavuoth festival when Jews traditionally eat dairy dishes. Sure enough, all the tables in all the mansions were laden with all sorts of dairy delicacies, including plump blintzes filled with cheese and dripping with butter. How his mouth watered!

That evening, he told his wife of this succulent sight. But alas! Neither he nor his wife had enough money to buy cheese and butter. What could they do?
They pondered the problem for hours, finally deciding that if they had to do without blintzes this year, next year, God willing, they would not be so deprived. But how?

Every day, the melamed was going to save one penny of his pay and his wife would do the same from her profit on the sale of her geese. This "blintz money" would go into a trunk they had lying around the house. The trunk was mounted on wheels and they were going to empty it out, cut a slot on the left and on the right on the top and

Kuchen

(hayven-teig)

Dough

1 envelope dry yeast or 1 compressed cake
¼ cup lukewarm milk
1 tablespoon plus ¾ cup sugar
1 cup scalded milk
1 teaspoon salt
1 cup butter, room temperature
2 eggs, beaten
5 cups sifted, all-purpose flour

1 Dissolve yeast in lukewarm milk. Add 1 tablespoon sugar and set aside.
2 Combine the scalded milk with the ¾ cup sugar and the salt. Add the butter and stir until butter is melted. Set aside to cool.
3 Add yeast to butter mixture and beat until smooth. Add the eggs and mix well. Stir in the sifted flour, 2½ cups at a time. Mix until dough is smooth and pliable.
4 Turn dough onto lightly floured board and knead for 5 minutes. Shape into a ball, transfer to a bowl and cover with a damp cloth. Let rise in a warm place until double in bulk, about 1 hour.
5 See opposite page for filling.

lock it up. Each morning, the melamed *would slip his penny through the right-hand slot while his wife put her penny in the slot on the left. Next Shavuoth they would unlock the trunk, buy flour, butter and cheese and feast just like the rich.*

The next morning, the melamed *put his penny in and so did his wife. But the following morning he said to himself, "I have so little money that I better keep it. Anyway, my wife's money will be enough by next year."*

Now, his wife was thinking along similar lines. "Why should I put my hard-earned penny in there?" she said to herself. So, both only pretended to put a penny in their slots every morning and both dreamed of eating blintzes. *Finally, a year passed and the great day arrived. With great excitement, they went over to the trunk, unlocked it, raised the lid and found — one penny under the right-hand slot and one under the left.*

"You cheat!" shouted the melamed *at his wife who screeched back: "You're the cheat! You wanted to eat* blintzes *at my expense!" Whereupon, the* melamed *smacked his wife's face, she grabbed the lapels of his coat, he pulled her hair and so on. The two continued fighting until both of them fell into the trunk with such a bang*

Fillings for kuchen

Cinnamon and raisin

1 recipe kuchen dough
½ cup melted butter
¾ cup brown sugar
4 teaspoons cinnamon
1 cup raisins

1 When kuchen dough has risen to double in bulk, punch down and place on lightly floured board. Roll out to ¼-inch thickness. Brush with half the melted butter.
2 Mix brown sugar and cinnamon together. Set 1 tablespoon aside for topping. Add raisins to main mixture and sprinkle over kuchen dough.
3 Roll up dough as for a jelly roll and divide in 2 parts. Place each roll in a well-greased tube pan, cover with a damp cloth and let rise in a warm place until doubled, about 1 hour.
4 Preheat oven to moderate (350°F.).
5 Brush kuchen with remainder of melted butter and sprinkle lightly with reserved sugar and cinnamon. Bake 35 minutes or until top is well browned.
Makes 2 cakes
Color plate facing page 145.

Apple

1 recipe kuchen dough
9 tart apples, peeled, cored and sliced
6 tablespoons brown sugar
2 teaspoons cinnamon
¼ cup butter, cut into small pieces

1 When kuchen dough has risen to double in bulk, punch down and separate into 3 equal parts. Spread each section on a greased 9-inch pie plate.
2 Place apple slices into the dough in neat, vertical rows. Mix the sugar with the cinnamon and sprinkle over dough. Dot with butter, cover with a damp cloth and let rise in a warm place until doubled in bulk, about 1 hour.
3 Preheat oven to moderate (350°F.).
4 Bake kuchen 25 minutes or until top is golden brown.
Makes 3 cakes
Color plate facing page 145.

that the lid slammed shut — the trunk was locked!

The struggle continued as the wheels of the trunk began to move, rolled out of the open door into the street and down a slope until it reached the entrance to the synagogue and rolled in just as the Chelm congregation were saying the morning prayer.

You can imagine their amazement! Jumping on the benches in fear, they cried, "Devils! Evil spirits! Save us, save us!"

The women in the gallery began to shout and the children burst into tears. The Rabbi quickly began to chant a Psalm which is a certain remedy for all troubles, but when the trunk continued to move, he decided that the men would have to draw lots to see who would risk his life to open the trunk. The unfortunate man confessed all his sins, wrote out his will and only then did he get down from the bench and pry open the lid of the trunk. To the utter shock of everybody, out popped the melamed *and his wife, he pulling her hair and she clawing at his beard, both shouting and cursing each other.*

The Rabbi persuaded the melamed *to tell the whole story from start to finish. As soon as Shavuoth was over the town council convened and passed three resolutions:*

Stollen
(hayven strudel - stollen)

1 recipe kuchen dough (page 138)
1 cup candied fruit mix
1 cup almonds, blanched and chopped
¼ cup melted butter
½ cup confectioners' sugar
1 tablespoon oil
1 teaspoon vanilla
¼ cup milk

1 When kuchen dough has risen to double in bulk, punch down and work in fruit mix and almonds.
2 Divide dough into 4 equal parts and shape each part into a ball. Cover balls with a damp cloth and let rest for 15 minutes. Punch down and flatten each ball into an oval shape. Brush each oval with melted butter.
3 Place on greased baking sheet (or sheets) and cover with damp cloth. Let rise in a warm place until double in bulk, about 1 hour.
4 Meanwhile, preheat the oven to moderate (375°F.). Bake stollen 25 minutes.
5 Just before the stollen is ready to be taken from the oven, dissolve confectioners' sugar in oil, vanilla and milk, and dribble over cakes while still warm.

Makes 4 cakes
Color plate facing page 145.

1. There are to be no more trunks on wheels.
2. No melamed *shall live at the top of a slope opposite the synagogue.*
3. It is forbidden for a melamed *and/or his wife to desire* blintzes *filled with cheese and fried in butter at Shavuoth.*

●●●

Apple strudel
(eppel strudel)

Dough

2 cups sifted, all-purpose flour
2 tablespoons sugar
½ teaspoon salt
1 egg, beaten
¼ cup melted butter or margarine
½ cup water
melted butter

Filling

6 tart apples, peeled, cored and cubed
¾ cup sugar
1 cup chopped nuts
1 teaspoon cinnamon
dash of nutmeg
2 tablespoons bread crumbs
½ cup raisins (optional)

1 Preheat oven to moderate (375°F.).
2 Combine flour, sugar and salt. Mix egg with ¼ cup melted butter and add to flour mixture, blending well. Add a little water at a time until dough is workable. Knead for a few minutes on a lightly floured board.
3 Divide dough into two equal parts and set one part aside. Roll one section in a thin, narrow oblong shape. Brush entire surface with melted butter.
4 Mix filling ingredients together thoroughly. Spread evenly over the lower half of the dough.
5 Fold upper half of dough over filling and pinch edges closed securely. Place on a greased baking sheet, shaping into a horseshoe if necessary. Brush with melted butter. Repeat same procedure with remaining dough.
6 Bake 30-35 minutes or until crust is golden brown.
Makes 2 strudels

Shavuoth cheesecake
(shevuosdiger kayz-kuchen)

Crust

½ cup margarine
¼ cup sugar
1 ⅓ cups all-purpose flour

Filling

½ pound cream cheese, softened
⅓ cup plus 2 tablespoons sugar
4 eggs, separated
2 tablespoons lemon juice
⅓ cup flour
½ teaspoon baking powder
½ teaspoon salt

1 Preheat oven to moderate (375°F.).
2 Prepare crust by creaming margarine with sugar. Gradually add flour and mix dough until dry and firm. Let rest ½ hour.
3 Roll out dough to ¼-inch thickness and line a 9-inch pie plate. Prick with a fork and bake 15 minutes. Remove from oven and lower temperature to 350°F.
4 Prepare filling by mixing cream cheese with 2 tablespoons of the sugar, egg yolks and lemon juice. Blend well and stir in flour, baking powder and salt.
5 Beat egg whites until foamy. Gradually add remaining sugar and continue beating until stiff. Gently fold into cheese mixture.
6 Pour filling into pre-baked piecrust and bake 45 minutes.
Makes 1 cheesecake
Color plate facing page 81.

*Rabbi Joseph Loksh is
another of the "Simple
Simon" figures in Jewish
jokes. They say that it was
his custom to eat
kichelech every Shabbat
morning on his return
from the synagogue. On
one occasion, eggs had
become very expensive and
so his wife had not made
any kichelech.
When Rabbi Joseph came
home from the synagogue
and did not find the egg
cookies on the table he
called the Rebbitzin and
said,
"Where are the kichelech?"
"Winter has come and the
hens have stopped laying,"
replied his wife. "Eggs
used to cost one penny and
now they cost three pen-
nies per egg."
On hearing this, Rabbi
Joseph Loksh was filled
with admiration.
"Look at that!" he ex-
claimed, "How clever
those hens are! They don't
lay an egg for one penny
— but they do for three!"*

Egg cookies
(kichelech)

2 eggs, beaten
3 tablespoons melted butter
1 tablespoon sugar
1 ½ cups self-rising flour
sesame seeds

1 Preheat oven to moderate (350°F.).
2 Blend eggs with melted butter and sugar. Gradually add flour
   and knead well on a floured surface 5 minutes.
3 Roll out dough on a floured surface to 1/8-inch thickness.
   Cut into rounds with a glass and transfer to a greased cookie
   sheet. Sprinkle with sesame seeds and bake 30 minutes or
   until golden.
Makes 24 cookies
Color plate facing page 144.

P

Poppy seed cookies
(mohn kichelech)

2 eggs, beaten
1 ½ cups sugar
1 cup margarine
½ cup poppy seeds
4 cups all-purpose flour
4 teaspoons baking powder
1 teaspoon salt
¼ cup water

1 Preheat oven to moderate (350°F.).
2 Mix the eggs, sugar, margarine and poppy seeds. Gradually
   sift in flour, baking powder and salt. Add water, blend
   ingredients thoroughly and knead. Chill.
3 Roll out dough to 1/8-inch thickness on a well-floured
   surface. Cut into desired shapes.
4 Bake on greased cookie sheets 10-15 minutes or until golden
   brown.
Makes about 6 dozen cookies
Color plate facing page 144.

Homentashen, *small triangular cakes, usually stuffed with poppy-seeds, are traditionally eaten on Purim. In Yiddish, they mean Haman's pockets; in Hebrew,* Oznei Haman *or Haman's ears.*

An ancient Talmudic commentary says that when Ahasuerus commanded Haman to honor Mordecai, "Haman entered his house in mourning, with his head bowed, his ears clipped, his eyes dark, his mouth twisted and his knees knocking. . ." There were scholars who thought that this might be the source of Oznei Haman, *but others argued that then the Jews could have invented "Haman's eyes," mouth, heart or even knees. Why ears?*

So there were other versions too. One of them has it that the custom of Oznei Haman *began among German Jews over 300 years ago and spread from there throughout the Jewish world.*

There are some scholars who claim that this was originally a Christian custom. The Christians in Central Europe used to call good Friday, the Friday before Easter, or Sad Friday because this was the day Judas Iscariot was supposed to have betrayed Jesus to the Romans. According to the legend, Judas Iscariot committed suicide on the day of Jesus' crucifixion

Almond-raisin crescents
(roggelech mit rozinkes un mandeln)

2 cups self-rising flour
1 cup butter or margarine, room temperature
½ pound cream cheese, room temperature
½ cup chopped almonds
½ cup chopped seedless raisins
2 tablespoons sugar
1 tablespoon cinnamon

1 The night before, mix flour with butter and cream cheese and blend until smooth. Place in greased bowl, grease top of dough, cover and chill overnight.
2 The next day, preheat oven to moderate (350°F.).
3 Combine remaining ingredients for filling. Set aside.
4 On a floured surface, roll out dough to ¼-inch thickness and cut into 2-inch rounds. Roll out each round as thin as possible.
5 Fill each round with a level tablespoon of filling, roll as for a jelly roll and shape into a crescent. Bake on greased cookie sheets 15 minutes or until golden brown.
Makes about 30 crescents

Crisp cookies and tasty sweets are baked especially for Shabbat. Pictured clockwise: Poppy seed cookies, Egg cookies, both on (page 143) and Honey confection I (page 150).

by hanging himself from a tall tree. Suddenly, the tree sprouted ears — lots of ears. The Christians used to revile Judas with noisy rattles on Good Friday and eat stuffed cookies that they called "Judas ears."

Another version is that Oznei Haman originated as a result of a pogrom that took place in the Jewish quarter of Frankfurt-on-Main, Germany in the years 1614-1616. The Jewish community of who numbered 4000 to 5000 were persecuted by their Christian neighbors, despite the fact that they had brought economic prosperity to the town and were highly thought of by the Emperor. The Frankfurt town council passed a special law which imposed all kinds of humiliations on its Jewish inhabitants. They had to wear a special mark of identification on their clothing, they were not permitted to pass the city hall building, nor to walk in the streets outside the ghetto walls, except on business. They had to obtain a special permit if they wanted to invite guests and had to put up special signs to mark their houses, (the name Rothschild — a red sign — originated here). The anti-Semites of the town were led by a baker called Vincent Fettmilch who dubbed himself the "Modern Haman" and was always looking for

Raisin-nut crescents
(roggelech mit niss un rozinkes)

Dough

2 envelopes dry yeast or 2 compressed cakes
½ cup lukewarm milk
¼ cup sugar
1 teaspoon salt
½ cup melted butter
2 eggs, separated
1 cup sour cream
3 cups sifted, all-purpose flour
1 tablespoon cinnamon
1 tablespoon confectioners' sugar

Filling

2/3 cup chopped almonds or walnuts
⅓ cup raisins

1 Stir yeast into milk until dissolved.
2 Combine sugar, salt and butter. Beat egg yolks and add to sugar mixture. Stir in sour cream. Add yeast mixture and 1 cup of the flour. Gradually knead in remaining flour.
3 Separate dough into 4 equal sections. On a well-floured surface, roll one section into a thin, round pie shape. Cut into wedge-shaped pieces. Follow same procedure for other 3 sections.
4 Beat egg whites lightly until foamy. In a separate bowl, mix the cinnamon with the confectioners' sugar. Brush each wedge with egg whites and sprinkle with cinnamon-sugar mixture.
5 Combine filling ingredients. Fill each wedge, roll up as for a jelly roll and shape into a crescent. Cover, put in a warm place and let rise for 1 hour.
6 Preheat oven to moderate (350°F.).
7 Bake crescents on greased cookie sheets 15 minutes, or until golden brown.
Makes about 5 dozen crescents

145

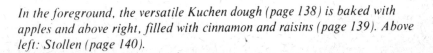

In the foreground, the versatile Kuchen dough (page 138) is baked with apples and above right, filled with cinnamon and raisins (page 139). Above left: Stollen (page 140).

new ways to oppress the
Jews.

One day in 1614, the
baker organized a mob of
ruffians and incited them
to carry out a pogrom on
the Jews. They attacked
the Jewish quarter when
the people were at prayer,
robbed and ruined the
district and drove the Jews
out of the town, leaving
their property behind.

It took about two years
before the Emperor of
Germany found time to
deal with the matter. Then
his army returned the Jews
to Frankfurt, arrested the
leaders of the pogroms and
executed Fettmilch. His
corpse was mutilated and
hung in the public square
as a warning to the
citizens, with its ears cut
off.

By the Jewish calendar,
this took place on the 20th
day in the month of Adar
which is six days after
Purim. The Jews of
Frankfurt called this the
"Second Purim" or the
"Vincent Purim" and used
to celebrate it every year.
Since Fettmilch was a
baker it may be that the
name Oznei Haman
originated in Frankfurt
after this event and then
spread to other places.

As to the name
Homentashen —
Haman's pockets in
Yiddish, there are people
who think that it was a
Jewish custom to bake
cookies for Purim, stuffed

Haman's pockets
(homentashen)

Pastry dough

2 ½ cups all-purpose flour
2 ½ teaspoons baking powder
1 teaspoon salt
½ cup sugar
4 tablespoons melted butter or margarine
1 egg, beaten
¾ cup milk
optional:
oil or 1 egg yolk
1-2 tablespoons water or milk
confectioners' sugar

1 Preheat oven to moderate (350°F.).
2 Mix together flour, baking powder, salt and sugar. Add
melted butter or margarine, egg and milk and mix in well.
Knead and roll out dough to 1/8-inch thickness on a floured
surface. With a glass or cookie cutter, cut out rounds 2
inches in diameter.
3 Place 1 teaspoon of desired filling (see page 148) in the center
of each round and pinch together three sides to form
a triangle.
4 If glazed crust is desired, brush *homentashen* with oil or egg
yolk diluted with water or milk. Put on buttered cookie
sheets and bake 30 minutes or until crust is golden brown.
Sprinkle with confectioners' sugar.
Makes about 40 homentashen

How to make homentashen

1 *Roll out dough, cut into 2-inch rounds and place 1 teaspoon of filling in center.*
2 *Fold halfway over and pinch 2 sides of round together, leaving center open.*
3 *Close up 3rd side by joining all sides together to form a triangle.*
4 *Brush with diluted egg yolk.*

with fruit, meat or cheese. Later they used to prefer them stuffed with poppy-seed which in both German and Yiddish is Mohn, *so they were called* Mohntashen. *But since* Mohn *sounds like* Homen, *(as they called Haman in Yiddish), they began to call them* Homentashen.
Some explain the poppy-seed filling thus: According to ancient legend, Queen Esther could not eat the food served in the palace of Ahasuerus because it was not kosher. So she ate seeds, which are permitted by Jewish law, and this is why we eat poppy-seed stuffing in our Oznei Haman.

●●●

Fillings for homentashen

Poppy seed

½ pound poppy seeds
2 eggs, beaten
2 cups sugar

1 Rinse poppy seeds 3 or 4 times in warm water until water rinses clear. Place seeds in saucepan with fresh water to cover, bring to a boil and simmer 2 hours. Rinse with cold water and drain very well until almost dry.
2 Add beaten eggs and sugar to poppy seeds and mix well.
Enough for 1 recipe pastry dough

Poppy seed, raisin and nut

½ cup seedless raisins
1 cup ground poppy seeds
½ cup chopped pecans or walnuts
1 cup milk
½ cup sugar
2 tablespoons melted butter
1 teaspoon vanilla

1 Soak raisins in water to cover for 2 hours. Drain and chop.
2 Combine all ingredients, except vanilla, in a saucepan and cook over a low flame about 20 minutes or until mixture is thick. Stir frequently. Cool. Stir in vanilla.
Enough for 1 recipe pastry dough

*The rich don't eat gold
and the poor don't eat
stones.*

●●●●●●●●●●●

*Sick people you ask if
they're hungry; healthy
people you feed.*

●●●●●●●●●●●

*If you live long, you eat
a lot.*

●●●

Chanukah donuts
(pontshkes-chanukah)

2 envelopes dry yeast or 2 compressed cakes
1 cup lukewarm water
4 cups all-purpose flour
½ cup sugar
1 teaspoon salt
1 egg, beaten
¼ cup oil
oil for deep frying
jam for filling
confectioners' sugar

1 Dissolve yeast in ¼ cup lukewarm water. Sift the flour with the sugar and salt, add dissolved yeast and stir in egg, oil and remaining ¾ cup water. Mix until dough becomes firm, adding flour if necessary.
2 Cover with a damp cloth, put in a warm place and let rise until doubled in bulk, about 45 minutes. Punch down dough, cover and let rise again.
3 Remove dough to a floured board and roll out to 1-inch thickness. Cut out 1½ inch rounds. Place on a floured cookie sheet, cover with damp cloth and let rise in a warm place until almost doubled in bulk, about ½ hour.
4 Fill a fryer or deep skillet half full with oil. When oil is very hot (but not smoking), fry donuts on both sides. Drain on absorbent paper.
5 Fill a cake decorator with jam and fill inside of each donut. Sprinkle with confectioners' sugar.
Makes about 24 donuts

Honey confection I
(honig tayglach)

4 cups all-purpose flour
2 teaspoons baking powder
6 eggs, beaten
½ teaspoon salt
2 cups honey
2 cups sugar
2 teaspoons ground ginger
½ cup chopped pecans or walnuts

1 Preheat oven to moderate (350°F.).
2 Sift flour with baking powder and salt, add eggs and mix well. Chill 15 minutes.
3 On a floured surface, roll dough into ropes ½ inch thick and cut into ½-inch pieces.
4 Place dough pieces on 2 greased, large, shallow baking pans and place in oven about 5-7 minutes, or until pieces are golden brown. Shake pan frequently to prevent pieces from sticking together. Remove from oven and set aside.
5 Combine honey, sugar and ginger in a 3-quart saucepan, bring to a boil, cover and simmer 5 minutes. Drop in dough pieces, add chopped nuts and simmer 5 minutes longer, stirring with a wooden spoon until *tayglach* are coated with honey and nuts are golden brown.
6 Moisten a large wooden board with cold water. Remove *tayglach* with a slotted spoon, transfer to the board and cool.
Makes about 120 tayglach
Color plate facing page 144.

Honey confection II
(honig tayglach)

7 eggs, beaten
4 ½ cups sifted, all-purpose flour
4 ½ teaspoons baking powder
½ teaspoon salt
2 cups honey
1 cup sugar
1 teaspoon ground ginger
1 cup chopped pecans or walnuts

1 Mix eggs with flour, baking powder and salt. Knead 3-5 minutes. Chill 1 hour.
2 On a floured surface roll dough into ropes ½ inch thick and cut into ½-inch pieces. Set aside.
3 Preheat oven to moderate (350°F.).
4 Place honey, sugar and ginger in a saucepan, bring to a boil and simmer, covered, 10 minutes. Meanwhile, heat 2 large shallow baking pans. Pour honey mixture into heated pans and evenly distribute pieces of dough.
5 Bake 20 minutes without opening oven door. Turn pieces over if necessary so that dough pieces become coated with the honey mixture. Continue baking an additional 40 minutes, stirring every 10 minutes with a wooden spoon to prevent pieces from sticking to each other and to the pan. *Tayglach* will be crunchy and dark golden brown.
6 Remove from pans and immediately sprinkle with chopped nuts. Cool. May be kept in a closed container indefinitely.
Makes about 1½ quarts

In the thirties, when Hitler rose to power, this joke went the rounds in Germany.
Hitler was inspecting a concentration camp and came across a Jew who was looking very worried. "What are you so worried about, Jew?" asked Hitler. "I'll tell you," replied the Jew. "We eat matzoth to celebrate Pharaoh's defeat and homentashen to celebrate Haman's fall from power. At Chanukah, we eat pancakes and donuts in memory of Antiochus' defeat so now, I'm sitting here worrying, wondering what we'll eat to celebrate your downfall."

● ● ●

desserts

desserts

*The famous philosopher
Moses Mendelssohn loved
sweets. One of his friends
was surprised and
commented, "Is it not
said, that fools like sweet
things."
"True," retorted
Mendelssohn, "that's
exactly what our
sages said, to make the
fools refrain from eating
the sweets so that they'd
all be left for the wise."*

●●●

Applesauce chiffon
(eppel-shnay)

2 pounds tart cooking apples, peeled, cored and quartered
1 cup cold water
2/3 cup sugar, or to taste
½ teaspoon cinnamon
¼ teaspoon nutmeg
2 egg whites
whipped cream
ground almonds

1 Place apples and water in a saucepan, bring to a boil and
   simmer until apples disintegrate, about 20-30 minutes. Stir in
   sugar until dissolved, remove from heat and cool.
2 Put through strainer or blender and mix in cinnamon and
   nutmeg.
3 Beat egg whites until stiff and fold into applesauce. Chill in
   individual serving dishes. Before serving, top with a dollop of
   whipped cream and sprinkle with ground almonds.
Serves 6

Prune and dried apple compote
(shabbesdiger kompot)

2 cups prunes
1 cup dried apples
6 cups cold water
rind of 1 lemon
1 cup sugar

1 Soak prunes and dried apples in water to cover, 1 hour. Drain.
2 Combine prunes and apples with rest of ingredients in a saucepan, bring to a boil, cover and simmer over a low flame until fruit is soft but still whole, 15-20 minutes. Remove fruit with a slotted spoon and set aside.
3 Continue simmering the liquid ½ hour. Cool. Pour liquid over fruit and chill.
Serves 4-6

Rhubarb compote
(rubarber kompot)

1 pound rhubarb stalks
1 cup sugar
grated rind of 1 lemon
2 teaspoons lemon juice
½ cup cold water

1 Wash rhubarb thoroughly, peel off any tough skin or fibers and slice into 1-inch pieces.
2 Place rhubarb and remaining ingredients in a saucepan, bring to a slow boil, reduce heat and simmer until tender, adding more water if necessary. Chill before serving.
Serves 4

Rice pudding I
(reiz-kugel I)

½ cup dried apricots
1 cup raw rice
½ cup sugar
¼ cup butter or margarine
4 large eggs, separated
½ teaspoon grated nutmeg
1 teaspoon grated lemon rind
¼ cup chopped walnuts

1 The night before, soak apricots in water to cover. The next day, drain and shred into small pieces.
2 Cook rice according to package directions. Cool and transfer to a mixing bowl.
3 Preheat oven to moderate (350°F.).
4 Cream sugar with butter or margarine. Beat in egg yolks one at a time, stirring well after each addition. Stir in nutmeg, lemon rind, shredded apricots and chopped walnuts. Add to rice.
5 Beat egg whites until stiff. Gently fold into rice mixture.
6 Pour into greased casserole dish and bake, uncovered, 45 minutes.
Serve hot or cold.
Serves 6

Rice pudding II
(reiz-kugel II)

½ cup seedless raisins
¾ cup raw rice
1 ½ quarts milk
½ cup sugar
pinch of salt
¼ teaspoon grated nutmeg
1 teaspoon vanilla extract

1 Preheat oven to slow (300°F.).
2 Soak raisins in water to cover. Set aside.
3 Combine rice, milk, sugar and salt. Pour into a greased, 8-cup casserole dish and bake, uncovered, 1 ½ hours. Stir every ½ hour.
4 Drain raisins and mix with nutmeg and vanilla. Remove rice mixture from oven and stir in raisins. Return to oven and bake additional ½ hour.
Serves 6

desktops

*Why is a poor tailor for-
bidden to eat cream?
Because buttermilk is
good enough for him.*

Soufflé
(offloyt)

3 eggs, separated
½ cup plus 1 tablespoon sugar
3 tablespoons butter, softened
3 tablespoons flour
¼ teaspoon salt
1 cup milk
filling (see below)

1 Preheat oven to moderate (375°F.).
2 Beat egg yolks with ½ cup sugar and the butter. Add the flour and salt and beat until smooth.
3 Bring the milk to a boil in top of a double boiler. Reduce heat, stir in egg yolk mixture and add filling. Remove from heat and cool.
4 Beat the egg whites with 1 tablespoon sugar until stiff. Do not overheat. Fold the whites gently into the egg yolk mixture with a rubber spatula or wooden spoon.
5 Pour into a greased soufflé or casserole dish and bake 30-40 minutes. Serve immediately.
   Serves 4-6.

Soufflé fillings

Apple

2 tart apples
1 tablespoon sugar
½ teaspoon cinnamon

Peel, core and grate apples. Stir in sugar and cinnamon and gradually add to egg yolk mixture in step 3. Apple soufflé may be sprinkled with confectioners' sugar.

Coffee

½ cup cold strong coffee
2 tablespoons flour

During step 3, stir coffee and flour into egg yolk mixture. Coffee soufflé may be sprinkled with confectioners' sugar immediately after baking.

Orange

Grate the rind of an orange. Peel off remaining white skin and discard. Dice the orange. Stir grated rind and orange cubes into egg yolk mixture during step 3.

Radish and honey sweet
(eingemachtz)

1½ pounds large radishes, peeled and chopped
½ cup whole almonds
1 cup honey
1 cup sugar
1½ tablespoons ground ginger

1 Place radishes in a 2-quart saucepan and barely cover with cold water. Bring to a boil, cover and simmer 10 minutes. Drain.
2 Meanwhile, blanch almonds by covering with boiling water. Let stand 5-10 minutes and drain. Remove skins, sliver and set aside.
3 Add honey and sugar to drained radishes in saucepan and shake until radishes are well coated. Bring to a boil and simmer 10 minutes or until sugar and honey are well blended. Turn up heat every 5 minutes for 30-35 minutes or until syrup has been absorbed. Mixture should be thick and golden.
4 Remove from heat and stir slivered almonds and ginger into radish mixture with wooden spoon. Cool slightly and pack into a clean pint jar. Do not cover until cold. Store in a cool place.
Note: This snack is of Balkan and Turkish derivation and is usually served in small dishes and eaten with a spoon while drinking tea.
Makes 1 pint

pesach

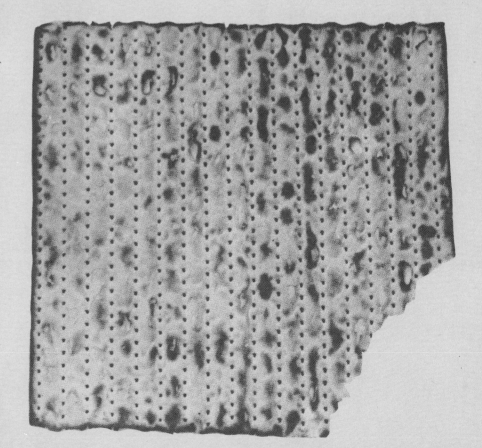

On Pesach eve a Jew went in to see the Hassidic Rabbi Yosha Ber of Brisk and asked, "Rabbi, every Jew is supposed to drink four glasses of wine at the Seder. Can I drink four glasses of milk instead?"
"Are you sick, God forbid?" asked the Rabbi.
"No, I'm perfectly well, thank God," came the reply, "but I can't afford the price of wine."
The Rabbi called his wife and told her to give the man a loan of 25 roubles, so that he could buy wine for the Seder. When the man thanked them and went away, the Rebbitzin asked her husband, "Why did you give him 25 roubles? Two roubles would have been enough for wine."
"I understood that he needed more than the wine from the way he asked his question," said the Rabbi, "for he wouldn't have asked if he could drink milk if he had meat for the meal."

●●●

Matzo meal chicken
(pesachdige hendel)

1 broiling chicken, cut into serving pieces
1 egg, beaten
½ cup water
½ teaspoon salt
2 cups matzo meal seasoned with pepper and paprika
oil

1 Preheat oven to medium (375°F.).
2 Dip chicken pieces in beaten egg mixed with water and salt. Coat with seasoned matzo meal. Make sure batter sticks to chicken by firmly patting on all sides. Place chicken pieces in baking pan liberally greased with oil and bake 35-45 minutes.
Serves 4-6
Color plate facing page 129.

On Seder night, after the feast and before reading the verses "Pour out Thy wrath . . .", it is customary to open the front door of the house. Some say that the reason for this custom is to invite Elijah the Prophet to come in and herald the arrival of the Messiah. Another version is that this custom was introduced in the Middle Ages, when they used to open the door to make sure that there were no anti-Semites lurking outside.

One Pesach eve the Jewish community of Warsaw sent matzoth, wine and other Pesach delicacies to the Jewish prisoners in the city jail. When the Shammes (beadle) went to collect the empty dishes after Pesach, he asked the prisoners how the Seder had gone off.

"Not quite," answered an elderly prisoner.

"What do you mean — not quite?" asked the Shammes.

"Well, we ate matzoth, we tasted the charosis, we drank four glasses of wine and we read the Hagaddah right through," replied the prisoner, "but when we got to 'Pour out Thy wrath...' and wanted to open the door — no way!"

●●●

Carrot and prune casserole
(floymen un mayeren tzimmess)

8 large carrots, thinly sliced
½ pound prunes
¾ cup honey
½ teaspoon salt
1 tablespoon lemon juice
3 tablespoons margarine or oil
3 tablespoons matzo meal flour

1 Place carrots in saucepan and barely cover with water. Bring to a boil, reduce heat, add prunes and simmer until tender, about 15 minutes.

2 Add honey, salt and lemon juice to saucepan, cover and simmer 20 minutes longer.

3 In a small skillet, melt margarine, sprinkle with matzo meal and mix into a thick paste. Add to carrot mixture and stir until thick and well blended. Brown lightly under broiler before serving.

Serves 4-6
Color plate facing page 129.

*One day, Hershele
Ostropoler's neighbor
came in to complain about
the mice in his kitchen
who had eaten everything
up and he couldn't do
anything to stop them.
"I have some good advice
for you," said Hershele.
"Scatter some crumbs of
the* Afikoman — *the piece
of* Matzah *eaten at the
end of the Passover Seder
meal — next to the
mouseholes. According to
the laws of Pesach, as you
know, you mustn't eat
anything at all after the
Afikoman, so they'll stop
at that and leave the rest
of your food alone."
"That's all very well,"
replied his neighbor, "but
how will the mice know
this law?"
"That's no problem,"
retorted Hershele, "not
long ago the mice in my
school ate up a complete
volume of the Talmud!"*

Matzo dumplings
(matza knaydlech)

1 cup hot water
1 pound matzoth
1 medium onion, minced
3 garlic cloves, crushed
3 eggs, beaten
salt and pepper to taste
dash of ground nutmeg
1 tablespoon fresh chopped parsley
salted water
matzo meal flour (if needed)

1 Pour the hot water over the matzoth and steep 5 minutes.
Drain and squeeze out as much liquid as possible. Mix in
onion, garlic, eggs, salt and pepper, nutmeg and parsley.
2 Fill a large kettle with salted water and bring to a boil. Test
consistency of dough by dropping a small amount into
boiling water. If dough falls apart, add a little matzo meal
flour to the batter.
3 Form dough into small balls and drop into boiling water.
When dumplings rise to the surface, reduce heat, cover and
simmer 15 minutes. Serve with soup or meat.
Makes about 12 dumplings
Note: This recipe may also be used as a chicken stuffing. For
this procedure, delete steps 2 and 3.
Color plate facing page 129.

How to stuff a chicken

1 *With a sharp knife, separate the skin from the meat near the neck.*
2 *Lift skin with left hand while inserting fingers of right hand between skin and meat.*
3 *Continue to separate skin from meat with hands to the drumstick.*
4 *Beginning at the neck, lift skin and spoon stuffing under skin.*
5 *Push stuffing back towards drumstick. Repeat procedure until entire chicken has been filled.*
6 *Truss chicken with string starting at the drumsticks, crossing under the breast and tying over the wings.*

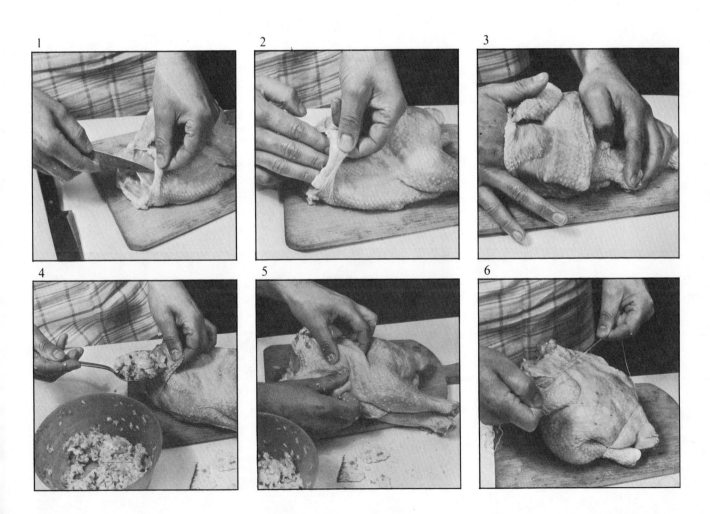

pesach

A poor man was once asked how his preparations for Pesach were getting on.
"Well, for the moment, I have completed the first stage of my preparations," *he said with a deep sigh.*
"What does that mean?"
"I've cleared out all the chametz *to the last crumb, but I haven't any matzoth yet."*

●●●

Matzo-apple pudding

(matza kugel mit eppel)

12 matzoth
2 tart apples, peeled, cored and diced
2 tablespoons shortening
4 eggs, separated
1 teaspoon cinnamon
½ teaspoon grated nutmeg
2/3 cup sugar
pinch of salt
½ cup coarsely chopped almonds

1 Preheat oven to slow (300°F.).
2 Crumble the matzoth and pour over water to cover. Soak for a few minutes, then squeeze out as much moisture as possible. Transfer to a deep mixing bowl. Add apples and shortening. Stir well.
3 Beat the egg yolks well and add cinnamon, nutmeg, sugar and salt. Add to matzo mixture. Stir in chopped almonds.
4 Beat egg whites until stiff. Gently fold into matzo mixture.
5 Pour mixture into a large greased casserole dish. Bake 1 hour, or until crust is evenly browned.
Serves 6

Rabbi Joshua Ber, the Tzaddik of Brisk used to say, "In the Pesach Hagaddah there are three things you must say; Pesach, matzoth and bitter herbs. It would seem that the order ought to be reversed; first the bitter herbs, which are symbolic of slavery, and then the matzoth, the symbol of freedom attained after slavery. However, our sages of blessed memory, deliberately changed the order for in order to realise the dreadful bitterness of slavery, a man must first taste the joys of freedom."

●●●

Baked matzo balls and prunes
(knaydlech un floymen kugel)

1 pound pitted prunes
boiling water
¼ cup almonds
3 eggs
3 tablespoons melted margarine
1 cup matzo meal
½ teaspoon salt
¼ cup raisins

1 In a saucepan, cover prunes with cold water, bring to a boil and simmer gently about 20 minutes. Set prunes in liquid aside.
2 Meanwhile, pour boiling water over almonds, let stand 5 minutes, remove skins and set aside.
3 Preheat oven to moderate (350°F.).
4 Beat eggs with melted margarine and blend in matzo meal and salt. Refrigerate 1 hour.
5 With wet hands, form into 1-inch balls. Press one almond and 2 raisins into each ball. Arrange balls in baking dish with prunes, pour prune liquid over and bake, uncovered, 40 minutes.
Serves 6

Pesach, you can eat where you like, but not what you like.
Succoth, you can eat what you like but not where you like. The best festival is Shavuoth — you can eat whatever you like, wherever you like.

●●●●●●●●●●●

A glass of tea and a chapter of Psalms can't do any harm.

●●●●●●●●●●●

You can't get drunk on tea.

●●●

Fried potato balls
(gepregelte kartoffel pletzlech)

2 ½ pounds potatoes
boiling salted water
½ tablespoon salt
2 eggs, beaten
3 tablespoons matzo meal
dash of nutmeg
oil for deep frying

1 Cook whole, unpeeled potatoes in boiling salted water to cover until tender, about 20 minutes. Drain, peel and mash.
2 Add salt, eggs, matzo meal and nutmeg to mashed potatoes. Mix until dough is well-blended.
3 Lightly dust hands with matzo meal and form dough into 1-inch balls.
4 In a deep skillet, heat enough oil to cover balls. Quickly fry potato balls until brown on all sides. Drain on absorbent paper.
Serves 4-6
Color plate facing page 128.

Matzo meal blintzes
(pesachdige blintzes)

Dough

3 eggs, beaten
1 ¼ cups water
1 cup matzo meal
½ teaspoon salt
⅓ cup butter or margarine

Filling

1 cup cream cheese (½ pound) softened
1 egg, beaten
1 ½ teaspoons sugar
½ teaspoon salt

1 Combine eggs, water, matzo meal and salt. Mix well.
2 Heat a small skillet and brush it with a small amount of the fat. For each blintz, pour enough batter to thinly coat pan bottom and tilt immediately so that batter spreads over the entire bottom surface of the pan. Lightly brown one side of the blintz and slide it out onto a towel, cooked side up.
3 Prepare the filling by mixing all the ingredients until smooth.
4 With cooked side up, place 1 heaping tablespoon of the filling in the center of each blintz and gently fold the sides over to form an envelope, being careful not to crack the blintz.
5 Heat the remaining butter or margarine in a large skillet and sauté blintzes on both sides until golden brown. Top with sour cream, honey or confectioners' sugar.
Note: Because of the coarseness of the matzo meal, these blintzes will be thick.
Makes 8 blintzes

pesach

When a poor man was dying, everyone used to bring him delicacies. Since by then it was too late for him to enjoy them, they would say: The poor man dies with jam in his mouth.

●●●

Matzo meal pancakes I
(chremzlech I)

1 cup matzo meal
1 tablespoon sugar
¼ teaspoon salt
1 ½ cups hot milk
4 eggs, separated
½ cup oil

1 In a bowl combine matzo meal, sugar and salt. Stir in hot milk. Cool slightly.
2 Beat egg yolks and mix with matzo meal mixture.
3 Beat egg whites until stiff. Fold into matzo meal mixture.
4 Heat oil in a large skillet and drop batter by the serving spoonful. Fry on both sides until golden brown. Serve with jelly, prune jam or confectioners' sugar.
Variation: Fry freshly made or leftover pancakes in melted butter with sliced bananas and top with brown sugar.
Makes 8 thick pancakes

Matzo meal pancakes II
(chremzlech II)

½ cup matzo meal
1 tablespoon sugar
½ teaspoon salt
¾ cup water or milk
3 eggs, separated
oil

1 Mix together matzo meal, sugar and salt. Stir in water or milk, beat in egg yolks and let rest 10-15 minutes.
2 Beat egg whites until stiff. Gently fold into matzo meal mixture.
3 Pour ¼-inch layer of oil into a large skillet. When oil is hot, drop batter in by the tablespoonful. Brown on both sides. Drain on absorbent paper towels. Keep pancakes warm by placing in slow (200°F.) oven. Serve with jam, or sprinkle with confectioners' sugar.
Makes 5 thick pancakes

Matzo pancakes III
(chremzlech III)

10 matzoth
1 cup matzo meal
¾ cup sugar
¼ teaspoon salt
grated rind of 1 lemon
pinch of ground ginger
5 eggs, separated
butter or margarine

1 Crush the matzoth in a bowl, cover with water and let stand 5 minutes. Squeeze out thoroughly.
2 Mix matzoth with the matzo meal, sugar, salt, grated lemon rind and ginger. Beat egg yolks and stir into the matzo mixture.
3 Beat egg whites until stiff. Fold into the matzo mixture.
4 Heat fat in a large skillet and drop batter by the tablespoonful. Fry both sides until golden brown. Garnish with jelly, jam or confectioners' sugar.
Makes 2 dozen pancakes

Apple-nut paste
(charosis)

1 large tart apple, peeled
½ cup finely chopped pecans, walnuts or almonds
1-2 tablespoons sweet red wine
1 tablespoon sugar
½ teaspoon cinnamon

Grate apple finely and mix with remaining ingredients until smooth.
Makes 1 cup or more

If you don't eat the maror *first, you won't get the* knaydlech *later.*

The miser would have his stomach cut out, if the operation were not so expensive.

Why did God turn Lot's wife into a pillar of salt? Because you can't turn a woman into sugar.

Carrot almond cake
(mandeln un mayeren tort)

8 eggs
1 ¾ cups sugar
juice of 1 lemon
1 pound carrots, grated
2 cups finely grated almonds
1 tablespoon matzo meal

1 Preheat oven to moderate (350°F.).
2 Beat the eggs with the sugar and lemon juice until fluffy and lemon colored.
3 Add carrots and almonds to eggs and mix in matzo meal. Gently mix until well blended.
4 Grease an 8 x 10-inch cake pan and pour in batter to ¾ full. Bake 30-45 minutes.
Makes 1 cake

One man has food but not appetite; another has a good appetite but no food.

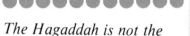

Eat what you like and wear what others like.

The Hagaddah is not the most important thing; it's the knaydlech!

Sponge cake
(tort — playva)

6 eggs, separated
dash of salt
rind and juice of ½ lemon
½ cup sugar
½ cup matzo meal flour
½ cup potato flour

1 Preheat oven to moderate (350°F.).
2 Beat egg yolks with salt, lemon rind and juice and half the sugar until lemon colored. Gradually mix in matzo meal flour and potato flour.
3 Beat egg whites until fluffy. Add remaining sugar a spoonful at a time and continue beating until egg whites are stiff but not dry. Carefully fold into egg yolk mixture.
4 Pour batter into a greased 8 x 10-inch cake pan and bake 35-45 minutes.
Makes 1 cake

Nut sponge cake
(nuss-tort)

6 eggs, separated
1 cup sugar
pinch of salt
1 teaspoon grated lemon rind
1 tablespoon lemon juice
½ cup matzo meal flour
1 ½ teaspoons potato flour
1 cup chopped nuts

1 Preheat oven to moderate (325°F.).
2 Beat egg yolks with the sugar and salt until thick. Stir in grated lemon rind and juice, add matzo meal flour and potato flour and blend thoroughly. Lightly grease a 10-inch tube pan.
3 Beat egg whites until stiff and gently fold into egg yolk mixture. Lightly stir in nuts. Pour batter into prepared pan and bake 45 minutes or until a toothpick inserted in the center comes out clean. Invert cake pan on a rack to cool.
Makes 1 cake

Almond macaroons
(mandel makarones)

¾ cup finely ground almonds
4 tablespoons matzo meal
grated rind of 1 orange
4 egg whites
¼ teaspoon salt
3 cups confectioners' sugar

Method I

1 Preheat oven to slow (300°F.).
2 Combine almonds, matzo meal and orange rind. Set aside.
3 Beat egg whites with salt and ½ cup of the sugar.
4 Boil remaining sugar with 2 tablespoons water until sugar is thick and begins to harden. (Test by dropping a small amount of sugar in cold water; if sugar forms a ball, mixture is ready.) Remove from heat. While sugar mixture is still hot, add gradually to egg whites, beating well after each addition. Continue beating until cool.
5 Gently fold in almond-matzo meal mixture. Drop batter by teaspoonful 1½ inches apart onto greased cookie sheets. Bake 15 minutes.
6 Increase heat to 350°F. and bake 15 minutes longer or until macaroons are lightly browned.
Makes about 4 dozen

Method II
1 Preheat oven to slow (300°F.).
2 Beat egg whites with salt until stiff. Fold in sugar a tablespoon at a time. Carefully fold in remaining ingredients. Drop batter by teaspoonfuls 1 ½ inches apart on greased cookie sheets lined with brown paper. Bake 15 minutes.
3 Increase heat to 350°F. and bake 15 minutes longer or until macaroons are lightly browned.
Makes about 4 dozen

The Kosher Kitchen

The origins of **kashrut**, the Jewish dietary laws, are found in the Bible. Specific rules are given for the selection and preparation of foods which are not only "clean," but also "ritually correct." These foods are called kosher. The word commonly used in contrast to kosher is **trafe** which means unfit for food or not in accordance with Jewish tradition and requirements.

Kosher meats

The most important rules relate to animal meat. The Mosaic code differentiates between clean and unclean animals which are forbidden. This is mentioned as early as Noah who was commanded to load the Ark with seven clean animals, but only two unclean. Only animals with cloven hoofs who chew their cud are permitted; all others are forbidden. Among the unclean animals are the camel, the rabbit, the hare and the pig. Certain cuts of meat are also not allowed and must be removed. Although the Bible does not list specific characteristics for fowl, it does list twenty types that are prohibited, most of them carnivores. Most reptiles are also taboo. The Bible lists eight which can no longer be identified. Only fish with scales and fins are allowed; all others are prohibited.

Many of these taboos are symbolic of the integrity and destiny of the Jewish people. For example, the thigh tendon or "sinew of Jacob" which must be removed, commemorates the struggle of Jacob with the angel who fought with him until dawn. Jacob conquered the angel and on the order of God, was re-named "Israel," which means, "Thou hast fought with men and angels and overcome them." The angel touched Jacob's thigh at the sinew and caused it to slip, so that for a while the Patriarch limped. The symbolic interpretation of this incident is evident: Israel may be attacked, it can never be conquered.

Throughout the ages, many have tried to explain the justification for the preservation of the **kashrut** laws. Some say that they stem from ancient rituals; others cite their hygienic nature, while others feel that these laws, which set the Jewish people apart from all others, are vital for the unity and preservation of the moral character of the People of Israel. Whatever the original reason, all permissible meat must undergo a strict procedure before it reaches the table. No Jew may eat the meat of an animal which has died from disease, old age or accident. The animal must be slaughtered by a **shochet** (ritual butcher) with a kosher knife. Every precaution is taken to insure the animal a quick and painless death. For example, the knife, which is described in detail, must be razor sharp, without so much as the slightest nick, ridge or bump. The exact spot where the knife is to cut is minutely described to protect the animal from unnecessary pain. Any deviation makes the meat trafe. By making the slaughter of animals for food a religious rite, one of the basic teachings of Judaism is emphasized — prevention of cruelty to animals.

After slaughtering, the animal must be examined to establish that it was healthy, particularly in the lungs. If any growth whatsoever is found in the lungs, the meat is disqualified. Then, and only after the animal has been given a clean bill of health, certain prohibited parts are removed.

After this, the meat is ready to be made kosher at home. According to the Bible, blood is the animal's soul and is therefore prohibited. All possible blood is removed by soaking the meat in cold water for half an hour in a pail used only for that purpose. The meat is then removed to a slanted board so the blood can run down, thoroughly salted on all sides and drained for one hour. Although tradition called for the meat to be then rinsed three times, many modern housewives wash the meat thoroughly only once under cold water. Steaks and chops need not be koshered if they are to be broiled, but the juice that escapes in the broiling process is trafe. Liver undergoes a different procedure. It is sprinkled with salt, broiled and then washed in cold running water before it can be used. This precaution against eating blood extends even to eggs. A drop of blood found in an egg is considered an indication that the hatching process has begun and therefore the egg, which contains the active germ of life, is forbidden.

Separation of milk and meat products

The Bible repeats "Thou shalt not seethe a kid in its mother's milk" three times. On the basis of this verse rests a whole system of the separation of milk and meat which has been extended to include fowl as well. Traditional Jews keep separate utensils for milk and meat and use different tablecloths, dishtowels and napkins so that there can be no chance of mixing milk with meat. No food can be prepared with both milk and meat, nor can they be served at the table at the same time. After eating meat, it is forbidden to partake of dairy products until a certain time has elapsed, usually from three to six hours depending upon local customs.

Foods which contain neither milk nor meat products such as fruit, eggs or fish are called pareveh and may be eaten with either. Fruits must come from a tree at least three years old, a custom stemming from ancient Palestine which would insure a strong, healthy tree. There are no restrictions on dairy products, provided that the milk is from kosher animals.

Pesach

Some of the most important dietary restrictions relate to the eight days of Pesach, when the exodus from Egypt is commemorated by eating **matzo** or unleavened bread. During this time, not only bread, but all forms of leaven are forbidden. Anything suspect of a contact between grain and water (where fermentation begins) is out of bounds — and successive generations have put together a tight net of stringent rules on this subject. A single grain of barley that falls into Pesach food is considered a tragedy that defiles not only the food itself, but even the dish in which it is contained.

Before Pesach, every Jewish household must be cleaned from top to bottom. The original intention was to uncover and destroy every last crumb of leaven. The kitchen gets special treatment: Jewish households keep a separate set of pots, pans and dishes to be used only for Pesach. Any utensil that is used throughout the year which must also be used during Pesach must be first immersed in boiling water to be absolutely sure of its cleanliness.

The symbolic explanation is that leaven represents the sin and evil in men's souls. Because it swells up, it is also a symbol of empty vanity. And so the cleaning out of leaven on the eve of Pesach is also symbolic of man's spiritual purity.

For many years, great Jewish Biblical scholars dealt with the question of **kashrut,** laying down a long and detailed series of rules and precedents. In the **shtetls** (small villages) of Eastern Europe, a Jewish woman with a **kashrut** problem that she was unable to solve would take it to the rabbi — sometimes bringing the pot with the food in question with her. If she happened to be poor, and her family hungry, the rabbi would often make a terrific intellectual effort to find some precedent that would make the food kosher.

The special restrictions of **kashrut** contributed to the unique characteristics of Jewish cuisine. The Jewish housewife found her own ways to cook tasty and satisfying food while observing the rules handed down by the Bible.

Index

181

Weight (Approx.) Dry

grams	ounces	teaspoons*	tablespoons*	cups**	lbs.
14.2	$\frac{1}{2}$	3	1		
28.35	1	6	2	$\frac{1}{8}$	
56.7	2	12	4	$\frac{1}{4}$	
85	3				
113	4	24	8	$\frac{1}{2}$	$\frac{1}{4}$
142	5				
170	6		12	$\frac{3}{4}$	
200	7				
228	8		16	1	$\frac{1}{2}$
340	12		24	$1\frac{1}{2}$	$\frac{3}{4}$
454	16		32	2	1

Liquid (Approx.) Fluid

milliliters	fluid ounces	teaspoons*	tablespoons*	cups**	pints	quarts
5	$\frac{1}{8}$		$\frac{1}{3}$			
10	$\frac{1}{4}$	$1\frac{1}{2}$	$\frac{2}{3}$			
15	$\frac{1}{2}$	3	1			
30	1	6	2	$\frac{1}{8}$		
60	2	12	4	$\frac{1}{4}$		
89	3			$\frac{1}{3}$		
118	4	24	8	$\frac{1}{2}$		
148	5					
178	6		12	$\frac{3}{4}$		
237	8		16	1	$\frac{1}{2}$	
355	12		24	$1\frac{1}{2}$		
473	16		32	2	1	
946	32			4	2	1

* Teaspoons and tablespoons should be levelled off.

** When converting to the Continental System, allowances for weights of specific ingredients should be taken into account.

Comparative Temperatures

Fahrenheit	230	250	275	300	350	375	400	450
Centigrade	110	130	140	150	170	190	200	230